Handbook
of
Bible Lands

Handbook
of Bible Lands

Guy P. Duffield

BAKER BOOK HOUSE
Grand Rapids, Michigan 49506

Contents

List of
Illustrations

List of Maps

Foreword

A trip to the lands of the Bible can be one of the greatest experiences in a Christian's life. Reading or studying the Bible without definite reference to the geography of the lands referred to results in a tendency to think of the events described in a vague, impersonal way. The names and locations of rivers, mountains, cities, and lakes mean very little. Distances have no significance. The effect of the topography in each country is lost when not experienced. The Bible appears to be only a book of lessons and people, unrelated to places and things.

Of course, nothing is better than to actually stand on the sites mentioned, and view with your own eyes scenes described in the Word of God. Then, the Bible and the individual events described take on entirely new and significant meanings.

On my first trip to the Holy Land, as we stopped at the

various places of biblical interest, people would continually ask, "What took place here?"

The following year, in planning my first directed tour, I prepared a mimeographed syllabus and gave one to each member of the tour before the date of departure. This enabled them to have the biblical information at their fingertips.

Since then, many ministers and tour leaders have requested copies of the syllabus. Realizing the need for a more complete and yet concise handbook, the original work has been tripled in size. The helpful maps and the pictures (taken by the author) have been added to the syllabus.

Well over one thousand Scripture references are given in this handbook. A few places, not mentioned in the Bible, are included in the descriptions because of their close association with important characters or events. Over five hundred and fifty biblical locations have been indexed. Where the name of a place has been changed, due to occupation by various nations during its history, each name is given. Eleven countries in which Bible events took place are included in the descriptive material.

Whether you be the fortunate tourist, a student, or a teacher of the Bible, I trust that this Handbook will make your experience with God's Word more meaningful and blessed.

Guy P. Duffield

Mediterranean Area

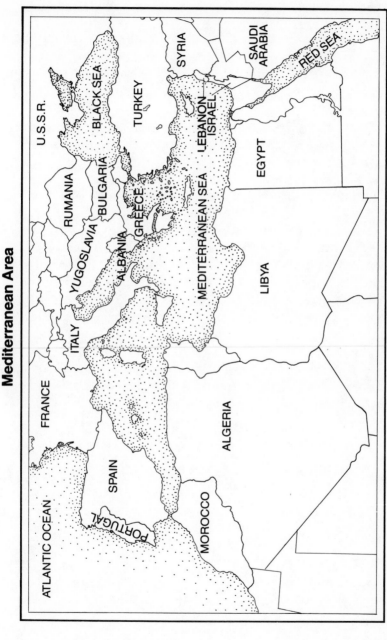

1

Cyprus

The island of Cyprus is located 60 miles west of Syria in the eastern end of the Mediterranean Sea. It is the third largest island in the Mediterranean, 148 miles long and from 15 to 45 miles wide. It is shaped like a fist with the forefinger pointing toward Antioch in Syria. Cyprus comprises about 3,572 square miles of land and has a population in 1982 of 635,000. It became an independent republic August 16, 1960, and a member of the United Nations in September of the same year. Its capital is Nicosia with a population of 160,000.

There are 1,000 mils in one Cyprus pound.

Cyprus is first mentioned in the New Testament as one of those areas, along with Phoenicia and Antioch, to which Christians fled as a result of the persecution which took the life of Stephen. They preached the gospel to the Jews wherever they went (Acts 11:19–21). It is also noted that some

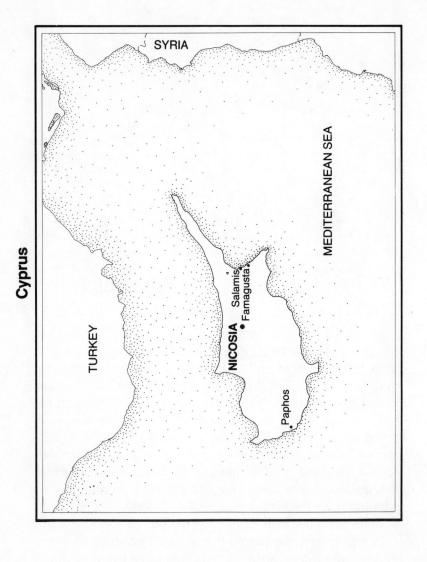

Cyprus

SYRIA

MEDITERRANEAN SEA

TURKEY

Salamis
Famagusta
NICOSIA

Paphos

Presidential Palace of the Archbishop and the Folk Museum at Nicosia, Cyprus.

Ledra Street, main business avenue of Nicosia, capital of Cyprus.

who came to Antioch from Cyprus and Cyrene (a city of
Libya in North Africa) preached also to the Greeks.

In the year A.D. 45 Barnabas, who was born on Cyprus, and
Paul set sail for the island on their first missionary journey
(Acts 13:1, 4). They landed at Salamis, the largest city on the
island, then some 3 miles from the present city of Famagusta.
It had a fine harbor which today is filled with silt. There was a
large population of Jews in the city as evidenced by the several synagogues in which Paul and Barnabas preached (Acts
13:5). Tradition says Barnabas later suffered martyrdom in
Salamis. A church in his memory was built there.

Leaving Salamis, Paul and Barnabas passed through the
island to Paphos, now called Baffo, on the western shore of
the island. It was then the capital of the Roman province of
Cyprus and site of the temple of Aphrodite, Greek goddess
of love and war. Here Paul preached to the proconsul whose
name was Sergius Paulus. A Jewish occultist by the name of

Bar-Jesus, or Elymas, withstood the message but was sternly rebuked by Paul and smitten blind. This miracle led to the conversion of Sergius Paulus, the proconsul (Acts 13:6–12). From here Paul and Barnabas sailed to Perga in Pamphylia (Acts 13:13), and then to Antioch in Pisidia; both are located in Asia Minor.

Because of a disagreement over John Mark, who had left them at Perga on their first missionary journey, Paul and Barnabas did not travel together on the subsequent missions. Barnabas went back to Cyprus with Mark while Paul chose Silas as his companion and returned to Asia Minor overland (Acts 15:36–41). Cyprus became a stronghold of the Christian church; this is shown by the fact that they were able to send three bishops to the Council of Nicaea in A.D. 325.

2

Egypt

The land of Egypt is one of the most fascinating countries of the Middle East. Side by side with modern development, one can observe people living, dressing, and working virtually as they did 3,000 years ago.

No nation ever had such a prolonged era of greatness. Beginning about 3000 B.C., when Upper and Lower Egypt were combined into a single nation, Egypt was the world's most magnificent civilization for the next 2,000 years. The spade of the archaeologist continues to reveal the marvels of those great days. The country possessed natural defenses, being bounded by water on the north and east, and almost impassable deserts on either side.

Appropriately called "the gift of the river," Egypt is situated around the Nile, a river whose many mouths form the huge delta which composes the country's northern section.

This delta stretches 150 miles from east to west, and about 100 miles from north to south.

Below the delta, Egypt is mainly dry and rainless except for a strip of green along the banks of the Nile that varies in width from 13 miles to only 1 mile at places and extends some 500 miles south. (A person can stand with one foot on fertile ground and the other foot on desert.) Of the country's total area of 386,200 square miles, only 4 percent is permanently settled.

The Nile's summer floods, from June through September, enrich Egypt's soil making it ideal for plowing and planting. These floods, which for generations were at the whim of nature, are now controlled by the dams at Aswân. The height of the river's flood has been recorded annually, as the chief event of the year, since at least 3600 B.C.

Vying with the Mississippi as the world's longest river (4,145 miles), the Nile is one of the few large rivers which flow north.

Because the visitor will hear constant reference made to events in Egypt's past, the following outline of the country's colorful history will be helpful.

In ancient history two Egypts have always been recognized: Lower Egypt, comprising the delta to the north, and Upper Egypt to the south, extending along the banks of the river to the first cataract at Aswân. Around 3000 B.C. these two were combined under an all-powerful god-king Menes who founded the first of the thirty dynasties which ruled Egypt until its conquest by Alexander the Great in 332 B.C. Egypt's history, to that point, largely centers around three Kingdoms with two Intermediary Periods.

Outline of Egypt's History

Early Dynastic Period 3000–2700 B.C.
    Dynasty I and II—Capital at Memphis (biblical Noph—Isa. 19:13; Jer. 2:16; 46:14, 19; Ezek. 30:13, 16.)

Egypt

MEDITERRANEAN SEA

ISRAEL

Alexandria

CAIRO •

Elat
Aqaba

Mt. Sinai

LIBYA

EGYPT

Thebes • Karnak
• Luxor

• Aswan

ANGLO-EGYPTIAN SUDAN

Old Kingdom—2700–2200 B.C.
Dynasty III to VI
During this time the great pyramids were constructed.

First Intermediary Period 2200–2000 B.C.
Dynasty VII to X

Middle Kingdom—2000–1800 B.C.
Dynasty XI and XII
Capital moved to Thebes (biblical No—Jer. 46:25, Eze. 30:14–16; Nah. 3:8).
This was the time of the artistic decorations of the tombs.

Second Intermediary Period 1800–1600 B.C.
Dynasty XIII to XVII
The Hyksos, Asian overlords, ruled from 1674–1567 B.C. (during Dynasty XV to XVII).

New Kingdom—1600–1100 B.C.
Dynasty XVIII to XX
The age of Egypt's supreme power and wealth.
During this time the children of Israel were in Egypt and the exodus took place.
Post Empire Period 1100–300 B.C.
Dynasty XXI to XXX
During Dynasty XXII Shishak ruled (1 Kings 11:40; 14:25–27; 2 Chron. 12:2–12).
During Dynasty XXVI Pharaoh Necho ruled (2 Kings 23:28–30, 30–35; 2 Chron. 35:20–24; 36:4; Jer. 46:2).
Persian Rule 525–332 B.C.
Alexander the Great 332–323 B.C.
Ptolemy I–XII 304–51 B.C.
Ptolemaic Period 300–30 B.C.
Cleopatra 51–30 B.C.
Roman or Byzantine Period 30 B.C.–A.D. 392
Conquered by the Arabs A.D. 600

Mameluk Period 1250–1517
Ottoman Period–Turkish 1517–1914
1805 Mohammed Ali appointed governor.

Egypt began its period of modernization.
1882–1936 Egypt occupied by the British.
1952 King Farouk, the last of the dynasty founded by Mohammed Ali, abdicated.
1953 Egypt became a Republic.
1954 Gamel Abdel Nasser elected president of the United Arab Republic.
1956 Suez Canal nationalized by Egypt.
1967 Start of long and intermittent Arab-Israeli War.
1970 Anwar el-Sadat is elected successor to Nasser.
1981 Sadat is assassinated. Hosni Mubaruk is elected president.
1983 Resumption of trade relations with Jordan.

Egypt in the Bible

Mizraim (Gen. 10:6, 13; 1 Chron. 1:8, 11) refers to ancient Egypt. Isaiah, Jeremiah, and Ezekiel have extended references to Egypt in their prophecies. The country occupies an important place in the history of the Bible, through its influence upon the children of Israel and its special relationship to four men:

Abraham went to Egypt during the famine not long after his migration to the land of Canaan (Gen. 12:10–20). Only the goodness of God protected his wife from being taken by Pharaoh. Abraham came out of Egypt with great riches in livestock.

Joseph was sold as a slave into Egypt (Gen. 37:36) where he served in the house of Potiphar (Gen. 39:1–20), experienced imprisonment (Gen. 39:21–40:23), was later exalted by Egypt's ruler (Gen. 41), and eventually revealed himself to his brethren after his dreams had been amazingly fulfilled

(Gen. 42–45). Jacob and his family then moved to Egypt where he spent his last 17 years in the land of Goshen, located at the southeastern edge of the Nile Delta (Gen. 46, 47). Joseph gave commandments concerning the carrying of his bones out of Egypt (Gen. 50:22–26; Exod. 13:19; Josh. 24:32; Heb. 11:22).

Moses was born in Egypt during the oppression—usually believed to be during the long reign of Ramses II. He was marvelously preserved and prepared for the work God had for him. After forty years on the desert of Sinai he was called to lead the children of Israel out of Egypt (Exod. 1–14).

Jesus was taken by Mary and Joseph to Egypt in response to the visitation of an angel of the Lord, that He might escape the wrath of Herod (Matt. 2:13–15) and also that Scripture might be fulfilled (Hos. 11:1). Visitors to Old Cairo are shown the cave under the Church of St. Sargius, an old Coptic Orthodox church built in the fifth century, where it is said the holy family lived while in Egypt. In time the angel of the Lord directed them back to the land of Israel where they settled in Nazareth (Matt. 2:19–23).

Places of Interest

Memphis—About 14 miles south of Cairo is Memphis, the oldest capital of Egypt, and its capital during most of its earliest history. Long since buried, it dates back to before 3000 B.C. However, interesting items are being unearthed by the spade of the archaeologist, including the alabaster sphinx and the huge image of Ramses II. Memphis is biblical **Noph** (Isa. 19:13; Jer. 2:16, 46:14, 19; Ezek. 30:13).

Sakkara—This is the mortuary temple complex of King Djoser. There is a 37-acre walled enclosure centered around the Step Pyramid of Djoser, the oldest of known pyramids (dating back to 2700 B.C.). In this vast area are the graves of more than twenty kings and hundreds of nobles. The Step

Pyramid is probably the oldest free-standing building of cut stone in the world.

The **Serapeum**—These tombs of the sacred Apis bulls which were worshiped at Memphis are 35 feet beneath the ground; they are 15 feet wide, 1,200 feet long in the form of a semicircle. The granite sarcophagi of 24 of these sacred bulls were found here.

The **Pyramids of Giza**—The three largest of these pyramids are those of Cheops, his son Chephrun and his son Mycerinus. Cheops, the largest of all, is the burial place of King Cheops and one of the seven wonders of the ancient world. It now stands 455 feet high, though once it was 481. Its sides are 750 feet long; each faces one of the four directions of the compass. The pyramid is made of approximately 250,000 blocks of stone weighing from 3 to 10 tons each—a total of some 5,400,000 tons. The base covers between 13 and 14 acres.

The **Great Sphinx**—Located near the Pyramids of Giza, this 66-foot-high sculpture faces toward the Nile valley. Carved out of the natural cliff, the Great Sphinx is the oldest of its kind; many similar monuments remain at Karnak and Luxor.

King Tut's Tomb—In 1922-23 English archaeologist Howard Carter broke through into the tomb of Tutankhamen and was amazed at the increadible riches there. The treasure, on display at the Cairo Museum, was discovered in one of sixty-four tombs found in the Valley of the Kings at Thebes (Tut's was the only tomb not robbed). Now known as Luxor, **Thebes** is the second oldest capital of Egypt; it is called **No** in the Bible (Jer. 46:25; Ezek. 30:14–16; Nah. 3:8).

Deir al-Bahri—This is the funerary temple of Queen Hatshepsut, who is believed by some to be the queen who

Queen Hatshepsut's Funerary Temple, Deir al-Bahri, at ancient Thebes, across the Nile from Luxor, Egypt.

reared Moses (Exod. 2:5–10). She was one of the first woman rulers of the world.

Karnak—Here, a short distance north of Luxor, is the site of another of the seven wonders of the ancient world—three temples originally covering an area of 100 acres. The oldest buildings date from 2300 to 2000 B.C. The great Hypostyle Hall, called the Forest of Columns, contains 134 columns 75 feet high and 12 feet in diameter. It is said that one hundred men could stand on the top of each. These columns are lavishly carved with the stories of the conquests of the Egyptian kings.

Cairo—With its mosques, bazaar, museum, and general appearance Cairo is fascinating to behold. The "City of the Dead," with its 15 square miles of buildings in which only the spirits of men are said to dwell is an unusual sight. In Old Cairo the Bible student will enjoy a visit to the Church of Saint Sargius. This is the oldest church in Egypt—a Coptic Orthodox church built in the fifth century. Under its altar is a cave believed to have housed Mary and Joseph and Jesus during their stay in Egypt (Matt. 2:13–15).

3

Greece

Greece occupies the southern tip of the Balkan peninsula in the eastern Mediterranean. It is bounded on the north by Albania, Yugoslavia, and Bulgaria, on the east by the Aegean Sea and Turkey, and on the west by the Ionian Sea. It comprises 51,200 square miles, slightly smaller than the British Isles or the state of Florida. Its population in 1982 numbered 9,800,000. The capital city is Athens with a metropolitan population of about 2,530,000. Ninety-eight percent of the people are members of the Eastern Greek Orthodox Church. Complete religious freedom is recognized, but proselytizing from and interference with the Greek Orthodox Church is forbidden.

The unit of currency is the drachma; there are 100 leptae in a drachma.

Of particular interest to the Bible student are the missionary journeys and ministry of the apostle Paul in Greece. He

and his party first came to the country on his second missionary journey, in response to the night vision he had while
in Troas. As recorded in Acts 16:9, he saw a "man of Macedonia ... saying, Come over into Macedonia, and help us."
(**Macedonia** is now the northern part of Greece.) Paul first
visited Philippi where he and Silas were cruelly beaten. He
then traveled along the Egnatian Way, famous military and
commercial highway, 33 miles southwest to **Amphipolis**
(now Neochori). Twenty-eight miles farther southwest he
stopped briefly at **Apolonia** (modern Pollina). An additional
journey of 40 miles along the Egnatian Way brought the
party to **Thessalonica** (now Salonika). After ministering
there and meeting much opposition, the evangelists traveled
50 miles south to Berea (modern Veroia). From here Paul
was conducted to Athens and thence to minister in Corinth.
He later returned to Greece on a subsequent missionary
journey.

Athens—Athens is in the southern part of Greece known
as Achaia (Roman name for Greece). In Paul's day Corinth
was the capital and chief city of Achaia although Athens was
the cultural center, being the seat of learning for the world.
The world's greatest university was here.

Athens is two miles from its seaport at Piraeus. In early days
the two were connected by two long parallel walls built two
hundred yards apart. Along these walls and throughout the city
were countless altars and shrines. It has been said that there
were almost more gods than men in Athens. Among its altars
Paul saw one dedicated to the "Unknown God." He used this
later as the basis for his sermon on Mars' Hill.

The city of Athens is built around the Acropolis, a rocky
prominence 500 feet high, on which were built numerous
temples. Visitors may see the famous Parthenon, the Erech-
theum with its famous porch of the maidens, the temple of
Wingless Victory and other ruins of the glory of Athens' past.

North of the Acropolis was the agora or market place.

Here Socrates taught and was forced to drink the deadly hemlock. In the agora the Athenians met to transact business and argue philosophy (Acts 17:17). It was here Paul entered into the discussions and "preached unto them Jesus, and the resurrection" (Acts 17:18, KJV).

At the northwestern approach to the Acropolis is Mars' Hill or the Areopagus, so named because it was here that the city court of Athens, called the Areopagus, met to decide matters concerning the city. On this rocky hill 377 feet high, Paul was brought that the council might hear more of the doctrine he preached. His great address, recorded in Acts 17:22–34, was delivered on this rocky hill. It stresses the facts that God is Creator, sovereign, and yet near to each person. He will judge all men by Jesus, Whom he raised from the dead. As usual, this great sermon had conflicting reactions: "Dionysius the Areopagite, and a woman named Damaris, and others with them (believed)" (Acts 17:34). As for the rest of the council, some mocked while others procrastinated, saying, "We will hear thee again of this matter" (Acts 17:32). Paul departed from them and went to Corinth.

Berea—After the uproar at Thessalonica Paul was sent by the brethren from that city. He traveled down the Egnatian Way to the city of Berea, about 50 miles southwest of Thessalonica. The city is known today as **Veroia.** Here Paul found a group of Jews "more noble than those in Thessalonica, in that they received the word with all readiness of mind, and searched the scriptures daily, whether those things were so." Because of this many Jewish and Gentile women accepted the gospel (Acts 17:10–14). Christian Bible study classes throughout the world have adopted the name "Berean" from the attitude of these people. Jews from Thessalonica came down and stirred up the unbelievers so that it was necessary for the brethren to send Paul away. He was brought to Athens. He probably revisited the church in Berea on his later trips through Macedonia (Acts 20:1–5).

Greece

Corinth—Situated 40 miles west of Athens on the narrow isthmus between the Peloponnesus and the mainland, the city of Corinth is 1½ miles west of the Corinthian Canal. It had two harbors: Cenchrea (Acts 18:18; Rom. 16:1) on the Saronic Gulf, an arm of the Aegean Sea; and Lechaeum on the Gulf of Corinth, an arm of the Ionian Sea. Ships from the east, Asia Minor, and Egypt used the former while the latter was the gateway to Italy and the western Mediterranean.

The Propylaea, Gateway to the Parthenon on the Acropolis at Athens, Greece.

In Paul's day there was no canal across the isthmus, although Nero, in A.D. 66, attempted to dig one, turning the first soil with a golden spade. It was a 200-mile journey around Cape Malea, with its treacherous and feared winds, and mariners found it less expensive to transfer their cargo across the 4-mile neck of land. Boats that were not too large were taken bodily out of the water and hauled across the isthmus on a roller-like skid structure, while cargos in boats that were too heavy for this operation were taken across the 4 miles and then reloaded into trustworthy sea-going vessels. Corinth prospered greatly from its strategic position in the center of all this trade. From 1881 to 1893 the project of cutting the canal through the isthmus, at its narrowest point, was completed. The ancient city lies just a short distance from New Corinth. This is a small city compared to the 500,000 people who lived in Corinth during

Paul's days. It was the capital of what is now southern Greece, called Achaia.

Above the city and to its south rises Acrocorinthus, a rock 1,887 feet high. Atop this rock was the temple of Aphrodite, the goddess of love. The temple was served by more than one thousand religious prostitutes who lodged in luxurious quarters surrounding the shrine. A large percentage of those who lived in Corinth were given over to the vicious and voluptuous practices of the worship of this goddess. Thus Corinth was the most notorious seat of immorality in the Roman empire. "To live like a Corinthian" became synonymous with a life of luxury and licentiousness.

The apostle Paul went to Corinth from Athens probably about A.D. 50 (Acts 18:1–11). It was then the most thriving, as well as the most sinful, city in Greece. Here Paul met Priscilla and Aquila who had come to Corinth because Claudius had expelled all Jews from Rome. Like Paul, they were tentmakers.

The first preaching took place in the Jewish synagogue. Crispus and his family were converted. Meeting severe opposition, Paul turned to the Gentiles, shaking his raiment as a testimony against the Jews (Matt. 10:14; Acts 13:51). He then preached in the house of Justus.

He ministered in this city for a year and a half. Paul's first epistle to the Thessalonians was written from Corinth. The two epistles to the Corinthian church are unique in their extensive instructive and corrective material concerning church decorum as well as the spiritual gifts and ministry. The judgment seat—Bema—is shown to the visitor today (Acts 18:12–17).

Patmos, Island of—The bare, rocky island of Patmos is in the Aegean Sea about 70 miles southwest of Ephesus and 37 miles from Miletus. It is about 8 miles long by 6 miles wide and comprises approximately 22 square miles. Patmos was used by the Roman government as a place for the banishment of criminals, who were forced to work the island's mines. The apostle John was sent there by the Emperor Domitian in A.D. 95 and it was while in exile on Patmos that

Part of the extensive ruins of Old Corinth showing the Temple of Apollo.

he received the visions recorded in the Book of the Revelation (Rev. 1:9, 10). The monastery of St. John on a rocky hill commemorates this event. Patmos belongs to Greece.

Philippi—Philippi stood about 10 miles from the Aegean Sea and its port city of **Neapolis** (modern Kavalla) (Acts 16:11). It was in the province of Macedonia, home of Alexander the Great. The town was named after Philip of Macedon, Alexander's father, located on the famous Egnatian Way, and became a Roman colony after the victory of Octavius and Antony over Brutus and Cassius on the plains outside the city. Ruins of the uninhabited site (called Felibedjik today) date from the second century, but the actual city of St. Paul's day has not come to light.

Paul and Silas came to Philippi on the second missionary journey in response to the call of the "man of Macedonia" (Acts 16:9). However, the first convert in Europe was not a man but a woman. Because there was no synagogue in the city, the Jews who lived in Philippi met for worship on the Sabbath day beside the Gangites River. Lydia, a business woman from Thyatira who sold purple cloth, accepted the message of salvation, was baptized along with her household, and opened her home for the members of Paul's party. Thus the first Christian church in Europe was established in Philippi.

As a result of casting out a spirit of divination from a young lady who daily cried after them, Paul and Silas were cruelly beaten and imprisoned (Acts 16:16–24). Miraculously delivered from their bonds, the apostles baptized the jailor and his household (Acts 16:25–34). The authorities of Philippi were deeply disturbed when they found they had inflicted violence on a Roman citizen (Acts 16:35–40). Paul left Philippi for Amphipolis, Apollonia, and Thessalonica (Acts 17:1).

Paul returned to Philippi on his third missionary journey as he returned to Jerusalem (Acts 12:3–6). The Philippian church was especially generous to him. (2 Cor. 8:1–6; 11:9;

Phil. 4:16–18). Paul's epistle to the church at Philippi was written from Rome while he was imprisoned.

Thessalonica—Thessalonica, now known as Salonika, capital of the province of Macedonia, is located at the head of the Gulf of Salonika. It is the principal seaport of southeast Europe. It is located 100 miles southwest of Philippi on the Egnatian Way which connected Rome with the cities of northern Greece. The city has a population of about 345,800. It was named by Cassander after his wife, who was a sister of Alexander the Great.

The Christian church was founded by Paul after he left Philippi (Acts 17:1–9). Here, in the synagogue of the Jews he preached for three weeks. Some Jews, many Greeks and a good number of "the chief women" believed. However, the Jews who did not believe influenced a base element to stir up a great disorder. They assaulted the house of Jason where the apostle was staying and accused Paul and his company of disloyalty to Caesar. It was here the well-known expression, "These that have turned the world upside down are come hither also," was used. Paul was immediately sent by the brethren away from the city, proceeding to Berea. Paul probably visited Thessalonica again, perhaps twice (Acts 20:1–4). He addressed the earliest of his epistles to the church there.

4

Iran

Prior to 1936 this country was known as Persia. One of the world's oldest empires, it has been called the "land of Sunshine, Roses and Poetry." It is the farthest east of the lands of the Old Testament, and occupies the western half of the Iranian Plateau which extends from the Indus River on the east to the Tigris River on the west. Iran is bounded by Russia and the Caspian Sea on the north, by Afghanistan and Baluchistan on the east, by the Persian Gulf on the south, and by Iraq on the west. The average height of the plateau country is 4,000 feet above sea level. The central part is a vast desert.

The capital of Iran is Tehran with a population of about 6,000,000. The total population of the country is about 41,450,000. It has an area of 636,293 square miles—three times the size of France. The monetary unit is the rial. Religiously, the country is almost unanimously devoted to the Shia sect of Islam—Mohammedanism.

In 1935, by official action of the Persian government, the name of the country was changed from Persia to Iran, which means "the (land) of the Aryans." The Medes and the Persians were the two Aryan tribes which came into the greatest prominence. The Medes occupied the northwest portion with their capital at Ecbatana (modern Hamadan). The Persians lived in the southeastern area. Cyrus built their capital at Pasargadae but it was soon moved by Darius to Persepolis in the south central part of the country. The other Aryan tribe, the Elamites, lived in the southwestern area of present Iran with their capital at biblical Shushan.

The following Scripture references refer to Persia and Media: 2 Chron. 36:21–23; Ezra 1:1–4; Esther 1:3, 14, 18; 10:2; Dan. 8:20; 10:1, 13, 20; 11:1, 2. The Iranian locations described here are of interest to the Bible student because of their relation to the Achaemenian clan: Cyrus, Darius, and Ahasuerus (Xerxes). Another city of importance is Abadan on the island of the same name which is at the mouth of the Shatt al Arab (the name of the combined Euphrates and Tigris Rivers which join about 100 miles north of the Persian Gulf). Abadan is notable because of its extensive facilities for the shipping of oil throughout the world. Shiraz, the capital of the province of Fars, is quite modern in comparison to the ancient cities of Iran. It is noted as the burial place of Iran's two great poets, Sa'di and Hafiz.

An important event took place in Tehran from November 28 to December 1, 1943, when President Franklin D. Roosevelt of the United States, Prime Minister Winston Churchill of Great Britain, and Joseph Stalin of the U.S.S.R. met together during a four-day conference during which plans were agreed upon for an all-out attack on Hitler's "European Fortress" in an attempt to bring World War II to a speedy end. They planned to defeat the German armies by land, their U-boats by sea, and their war plants from the air.

More recently, Iranian revolutionary militants invaded the

Iran

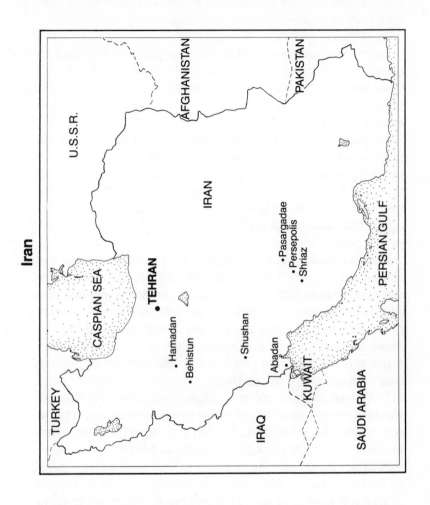

U.S. Embassy in Tehran on November 4, 1979, seizing staff members as hostages. They were not released until January 20, 1981, after 444 days of captivity.

Later the same year, President Bani-Sadr was ousted as president by once-exiled Ayatollah Khomeini. Bani-Sadr went into hiding and on July 24, Prime Minister Mohammed Ali Rajai was elected president, only to be murdered one month later.

In March 1982, Iran launched an offensive against its neighbor, Iraq, regaining much of the border area occupied by that country in the latter part of 1980. The two countries continue to be at war although Iraq is willing to stop; Iran wants certain demands met before ending the conflict. The fighting spread into the Persian Gulf in 1984.

Behistun—Behistun, or Besitun as it is called, is a village at the foot of a 1,700-foot peak in the Zagros Mountains. The old caravan road between Ecbatana (Hamadan) and Babylon passes at the foot of the cliff. Some 500 feet above a spring at the base of the rock Darius had inscribed an impressive autobiography of his conquests. One of his victories was accomplished near here in 516 B.C. The carvings depict the king lording it over his enemies.

The inscription is written in three languages: Old Persian, Elamite, and Akkadian. It was this trilingual inscription which enabled scholars to unlock the cuneiform script just as the trilingual Rosetta Stone provided the key to the Egyptian hieroglyphs.

Hamadan—Hamadan is the **Achmetha** of the Bible (Ezra 6:1, 2) where Darius found the record of Cyrus's decree allowing the Jews to rebuild the Temple at Jerusalem. The classical name of this city through much of its important history has been Ecbatana.

Ecbatana was the capital of Northern Media. Cyrus the Great held his court here.

Beautiful detail of a huge mosque at Isfahan in Iran.
Photo courtesy of Pan American Airways.

Typical Iranian Mohammedan mosque located at Isfahan, Iran.
Photo courtesy of Pan American Airways.

Pasargadae—Pasargadae is a city of ancient Persia situated in the modern Plain of Murghab some 30 miles northeast of the ruins of Persepolis. It was built by Cyrus to celebrate the victory which made him king of Media as well as Persia. Here he built his palace and the tomb in which he is buried. Darius later moved the capital to Persepolis.

Persepolis—Built by Darius I, Persepolis is the ancient capital of Persia. Located 40 miles northeast of Shiraz, the site is marked by a large terrace on which are a number of colossal ruins including many huge pillars still erect.

This city was captured and partially destroyed by Alexander the Great. The ruins used to be called **Sad-Sutun,** meaning "the 100 columns." They are now known as Takht-i-Jamshid. Here are found the tombs of Artaxerxes II and III. Not far from the ruins of Persepolis, at Nakshi-i-Rustrum, are the tombs of Darius, Xerxes I, Artaxerxes I, and Darius II.

Shushan—Susa, as Shushan is called today, was the capital of the province of Elam. It is located east of Babylonia, on the Karkheh River, 150 miles north of the Persian Gulf. Chedorlaomer, king of Elam in the days of Abraham, was one of the kings who fought against Sodom and other cities and took Lot captive (Gen. 14:1–11). There were Jews from Elam present in Jerusalem on the day of Pentecost (Acts 2:9).

Susa was called Shushan in the Bible during the time it was part of the Persian Empire (Neh. 1:1; Esther 1:2). Shushan was the royal winter residence of Darius the Great and was one of the three capitals of the Persian Empire. The great palace covered 20 acres.

The dramatic events of the Book of Esther took place at Shushan. Here Haman built the gallows on which he hoped to destroy Mordecai, but on which he himself was executed (Esther 5:14; 7:9, 10). The great deliverance which was achieved by the Jews through the intervention of Queen Esther, herself a Jewess, is celebrated each year by the Jews at the Feast of Purim (Esther 9:20–32). The Ahasuerus of the Book of Esther is the great Persian king Xerxes of secular history.

One of the most important discoveries to be unearthed at Susa is a black basalt pillar on which is inscribed the famous law code of the Babylonian king Hammurabi. Also to be seen at the site are the outline, and some of the beautiful glazed bricks of the splendid Persian royal palace begun by Darius I and enlarged and adorned by later kings.

Muslim tradition says that the tomb of the prophet Daniel lay in the bed of the Karkheh River not far from Susa. A mosque was built on the bank opposite the supposed spot.

5

Iraq

The modern country of Iraq, which was taken from Turkey during World War I, became a sovereign state at the end of the British mandate in 1932. It is made up principally of the land between the Tigris and Euphrates Rivers which was known in ancient times as **Mesopotamia** ("Mesopotamia" comes from two words meaning "between the rivers;" Gen. 24:10; Acts 7:2). It is bounded on the north by Turkey, east by Iran (formerly Persia), south by Kuwait and the Persian Gulf, and southwest by Saudi Arabia. The population of Iraq is about 14,000,000. Its capital city of Baghdad (with a population of over 3,300,000) is situated on the Tigris River. Baghdad is not mentioned in the Bible, being only about 1,200 years old. It is the city of the medieval caliphs and is known to the West through the "Arabian Nights."

The Tigris River, which is called Hiddekel in Genesis 2:14 and Daniel 10:4, is about 1,150 miles long. It has its rise in the highlands of Armenia in Asia Minor (now Turkey), and flows in a southwestward direction to join the Euphrates about 100 miles from the Persian Gulf. The combined stream is called Shatt al Arab. Though narrower than the Euphrates, the Tigris is swifter and carries much more water. On its banks stood the great Assyrian cities of Ashur and Nineveh. The ancient capitals at Babylon and Nineveh were once the greatest cities of the world. Opposite the site of old Nineveh, in northern Iraq, is Mosul, center of extensive oil deposits.

The Euphrates River has its source in the Anti-Taurus range of eastern Turkey near the Black Sea. It flows through Syria, then southeastward through Mesopotamia to join the Tigris at Basra. The river is navigable for approximately two-thirds of its 1,675 miles.

The Euphrates is first mentioned in the Bible in Genesis 2:14. It was "the river" (Exod. 23:31; Deut. 11:24) and "the great river" (Gen. 15:18; Deut. 1:7). God promised it was to be the northeastern boundary of the land given to Abraham and his seed. Only for a short period of time, during the reigns of David and Solomon, did Israel possess this extensive territory (2 Sam. 8:3; 10:16; 1 Kings 4:24). During the reign of Jehoiachin of Judah the Euphrates served as the dividing line between the spheres of influence of Babylonia and Egypt (2 Kings 24:7). The delta of the Euphrates ends at Hit, 400 miles upstream. At this place the elevation is still less than 100 feet above sea level. Thus the flatness of the area can be realized.

The Bible particularly mentions the cities of Ur and Babylon which were in what is now Iraq.

Babylon—The first reference to Babylon is no doubt the story of the Tower of Babel (Gen. 11:1–6). This tower, which the people of that day thought to build to heaven, may have been similar to the characteristic building of the Mesopotamia area called a ziggurat. This is a huge artificial mound made out of sun-dried bricks. There being no timber or rock

Iraq

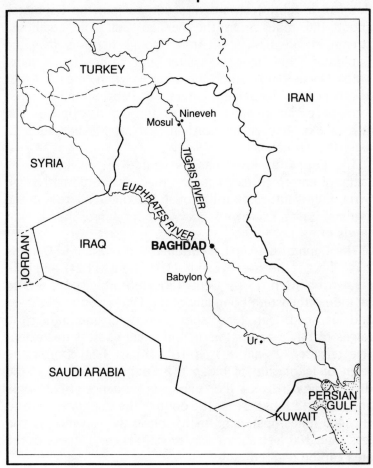

Ruins of Babylon, Iraq.

on the alluvial plain of Babylonia, the people devised the brick for their construction. Genesis 11:3 states, "Go to, let us make brick, and burn them throughly. And they had brick for stone and slime [bitumen] had they for mortar." More than two dozen of these mounds have been found in this plain. Some were mounds of clay well tamped down and buttressed on the outside by brick and bitumen. These were built in step-like stages. There were usually three stages with a temple to one of their gods on top. As many as eight stages have been built. The Tower of Babel, which may or may not have been a ziggurat, was probably built prior to 4000 B.C. Perhaps the others were copies of it.

"Babylon" comes from the Hebrew root meaning "to confound." Its original founding is attributed to Nimrod, "a mighty hunter before the Lord" (Gen. 10:8–10). The city began to rise in prominence about 1830 B.C., but did not reach the height of its glory until the reign of Nebuchadnezzar II (605–562 B.C.). He built huge fortifications, great streets which were laid out at right angles to each other, canals, temples, a ziggurat, and the famous hanging gardens. These were huge terraces on which were planted full-grown trees. The inner and outer walls of the city were said to be over 13 miles long on each side, 250 to 300 feet high and at least 80 feet thick; there were 100 gates, 25 on each side.

Babylon was more than a city. It was also a great empire which extended from the Persian Gulf to Syria and Palestine. It was the first of the great gentile world kingdoms represented by the image of Nebuchadnezzar's dream (Dan. 2:31–38). It was Nebuchadnezzar, king of Babylon, who destroyed the beautiful temple built by Solomon at Jerusalem and who carried Judah away to Babylon in captivity (2 Kings 24:11–25:21). The city of Babylon fell to the Medes and Persians (539 B.C.) as Belshazzar desecrated the sacred vessels taken from the temple in Jerusalem (Dan. 5).

Because of its iniquity God prophesied total and permanent destruction of the city of Babylon. Probably no other city of its prominence has suffered a more total extinction.

Famous Ishtar Gate reconstructed in blue tile on the site of ancient Babylon on the Euphrates River in Iraq.

Note the drastic judgments in these prophecies: Isa. 13:19–22; 47; Jer. 50, 51.

It was at Babylon that Alexander the Great died on June 13, 323 B.C., after a short illness.

In the Book of Revelation Babylon represents apostate Christendom or ecclesiastical Babylon, the great harlot. It also seems to represent the consummation of political power (Rev. 17, 18).

Nineveh—Nineveh was the great capital city of Assyria. Assyria proper extended from the Mountains of Armenia in the north to the lower Zab River in the south. Media was its east boundary and it extended somewhat into Mesopotamia on the west bank of the Tigris. At one time it was expanded to control the territory from the Persian Gulf to the Mediterranean Sea, including Egypt. The city of Nineveh was located

Huge building made of cane. Typical construction in ancient Mesopotamia, Iraq.

on the banks of the Tigris River about 200 miles north of Babylon.

To this great city Jonah was instructed to go. After his experience in the great fish, he obeyed (Jonah 1:1, 2; 3:1–10). The city with its environs was very extensive. It is called "that great city," and "an exceeding great city" (1:2; 3:2–3; 4:11). It apparently took Jonah three days to cover its territory (3:3, 4). Jonah 4:11 would seem to indicate that there were 120,000 who were too young to tell their right hand from their left, thus giving some idea of the total population.

Because of its repentance, Jesus said Nineveh was a sign to his unrepentant generation (Matt. 12:41; Luke 11:32). He also spoke of himself being a sign as Jonah was (Matt. 12:40; Luke 11:30). Though Nineveh repented at Jonah's preaching it was later destroyed in 612 B.C. by the combined forces of the Medes and the Babylonians. The prophecy of Nahum is concerned with the destruction of Nineveh. The following references from the Book of Nahum are most expressive: 1:8; 2:6; 3:13, 15.

The city of Samaria fell before the Assyrians in 722 B.C., and Israel, the Northern Kingdom, was carried captive to their land (2 Kings 17:3–6, 23). A later king of Assyria, Sennacherib, was not quite as successful in his campaign against Judah. During the reign of Hezekiah, king of Judah, he conquered much of Judah's territory but his forces were destroyed by the angel of the Lord as they surrounded the city of Jerusalem (2 Kings 18:13–19:37; 2 Chron. 32:1–21; Isa. 36, 37).

Ur—"Ur of the Chaldees" (Gen. 11:28, 31; 15:7; Neh. 9:7; Acts 7:4) was located on the Euphrates River in what is now Iraq. In ancient times it was the capital of the land of Sumer—called **Shinar** in the Bible (Gen. 11:2). Sumer once encompassed the territory from the Persian Gulf to the area above Baghdad. Sumer was forgotten until about 100 years ago. Now thousands upon thousands of clay tablets have been unearthed bearing man's oldest form of writing, called "cuneiform," from the Latin *cuneus* meaning *wedge* (the letters are wedge shaped). These tablets bear stories of man's creation and of a great flood inundating all of mankind except for one good man.

Ur was the capital of earth's first great civilization. Here the Bible, as well as history itself, had its beginning. There were chariots in those days, which go back to 3500 B.C. The wheel was in use in Sumer 1,500 years before it was introduced to Egypt by the Hyksos intruders. The Sumerians produced the sexagesimal system—numbering by sixties—which is still used in reckoning time (sixty seconds in a minute and sixty minutes in an hour) and in the measurement of a circle (360 degrees in a circle).

King Ur-Nammu, who founded the last great dynasty of Ur, is famous for having drawn up the oldest code of laws yet known to man—he did it 4,000 years ago. The great Hammurabi, who came from Babylon in the north to conquer Sumer about 1750 B.C., borrowed from Ur-Nammu.

Also at Ur may be seen one of the finest remains of a ziggurat—similar, no doubt, to the tower of Babel.

6

Israel

The nation of Israel is located at the eastern end of the Mediterranean Sea. It is bounded on the north by Lebanon, and on the east by Syria and the Hashemite Kingdom of Jordan. It has always been a sort of land bridge between the north, Mesopotamia, and Egypt. The country today occupies 7,992 square miles. Jerusalem is the capital.

Israeli currency is based on the shekel which is divided into 100 agorot (singular agrah).

Israel is a young nation, having been established May 14, 1948. Its founding was a dramatic one. In 1947 the British government announced that it would be giving up its mandate over Palestine in May of the following year. As a result, the United Nations in 1947 established a special committee to look into the situation. After considerable study they recommended that the country be partitioned into two states, one Jewish and one Arab, with Jerusalem becoming an international city. The Jews accepted the plan but the Arabs refused to do so, indicating that partition meant war. However, on November 29, 1947, the United Nations Assembly approved the recommendation. The Arabs were still opposed to the idea, and seven Arab nations surrounded the little Jewish area. To combat their combined armies Israel had only 35,000 partially trained troops equipped with a few thousand rifles, a few hundred machine guns, home-made Sten-guns, and a few dozen anti-aircraft guns and mortars.

As May 14, 1948 approached, the members of the "National Administration" under the leadership of David Ben Gurion searched their hearts and contemplated the wisdom of declaring a Jewish state. Their underground warned them of the impending attacks by land and air. The cities were defenseless and wide open to air attack. In the face of all this, less than forty-eight hours before the British Mandate ended, the majority of the council of thirty-seven members representing all political groups within the country voted for independence. At four o'clock in the afternoon of May 14, a few hours before the British had withdrawn, the ceremony began in which David Ben Gurion read the 979-word Declaration of Independence, while people throughout Israel and the world gathered around radios to listen. A nation was born out of antiquity after 1,878 years. That night Egyptian planes bombed Tel Aviv and the Arab armies marched into Israel.

The story of the "War of Liberation," as it is called by the Israeli, is one of unbelievable dedication—and miracle. The world's best military leaders gave Israel four to seven days to survive. The war raged for a year before an armistice between Israel and Jordan was arranged. The Arab peoples have never recognized the existence of the state of Israel; they refer to it as "Occupied Palestine."

The year 1956 saw another climax of increasing tensions between Israel and her Arab neighbors. Any hopes of calmer conditions were shattered by Egyptian nationalization of the Suez Canal on July 26 of that year. On October 29 Israeli

Israel

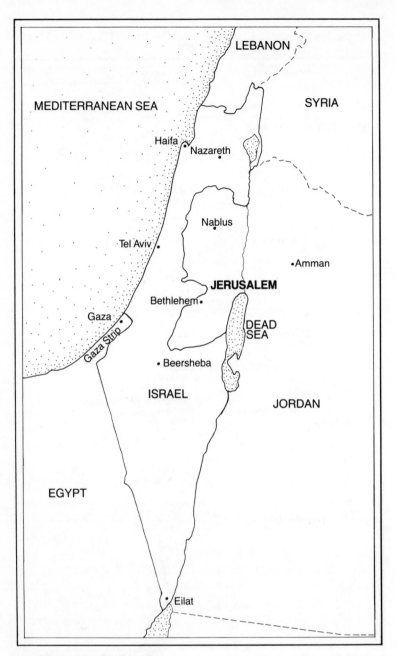

Israel before the Six-Day War

troops, recognizing that their main foe was Egypt, attacked the Sinai Peninsula and by November 5 occupied the entire peninsula, including the Gaza Strip, with the exception of a 10 mile cordon along the Suez Canal. Great Britain and France attacked Egypt in an effort to keep the canal open. This invasion lasted only a brief time as the United Nations requested Britain and France to withdraw. Israel also agreed to withdraw her troops to the 1949 armistice lines.

As a result of the Six-Day War in June of 1967 Israel extended her territory to include all of the Sinai Peninsula to the banks of the Suez Canal, the entire West Bank of the Jordan River, and the Golan Heights east of the Sea of Galilee. That territory changed in 1973 when Israel pushed attacking Syrians back beyond the 1967 cease-fire lines and recrossed the canal. And it changed again in 1974 when Israeli forces—by agreement—pulled back from the canal and Sinai Peninsula. (This withdrawal from the Sinai was completed in April 1982.)

Outline History of the Holy Land

The visitor to the Holy Land, unless he has made a detailed study of the history of the Middle East, will probably become confused as references are made to different periods in the long and varied past which this land has known. The following outline traces the main periods, with approximate dates, and will help the average person to better relate places and events to each other and to the whole amazing movement that has been transpiring for centuries past.

Pre-Biblical Period 9000–2000 B.C.

Archaeologists tell us that the Holy Land was occupied as early as 9000 B.C. If this is true, these would be the oldest known communities on earth. During the last millenium of that time, 3000–2000 B.C., Palestine was in close contact with Egypt.

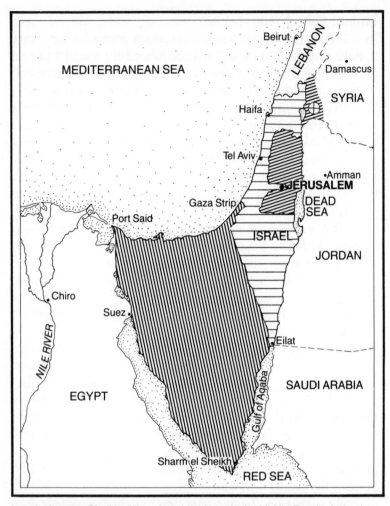

Israel after the Six-Day War—Israel said war in the Middle East had wiped out past armistice pacts and indicated borders would have to change. Area overrun by Israeli forces is shown in light shading. Cease-fire in the Syrian area (cross) was accepted. The Sinai Peninsula (large shaded area in the lower portion of the map) was returned to Egypt, by Israel, on April 20, 1982.

48

Biblical Period 1900–721 B.C.

1900 B.C. Abraham arrives in Canaan from Mesopotamia. Palestine is held by the Hyksos (shepherd kings) of Egypt until 1479 when defeated by Thothmes III at Megiddo. Palestine would be part of Egypt for the next 400 years.

1630 B.C. Jacob and his family go to Egypt during the great famine to be with Joseph.

1250 B.C. Joshua crosses the Jordan and conquers Palestine, dividing it among the twelve tribes.

1200 B.C. The Philistines' invasion from Crete.

1100 B.C. They occupy all Palestine by 1050 B.C. Samson is killed.

1064 B.C. Saul is crowned the first king of Israel. He is slain at Mount Gilboa in 1004 B.C.

1004–965 B.C. David's reign.

965–922 B.C. Solomon's reign. The Temple is dedicated about 953 B.C.

930 B.C. Israel is divided into Northern and Southern Kingdoms—Israel and Judah.

721 B.C. Assyrians capture Samaria and take Israel (ten northern tribes) into captivity, marking the end of that kingdom.

Babylonian Period 605–562 B.C.

587 B.C. Nebuchadnezzar captures and destroys Jerusalem, carrying Judah into captivity to Babylon.

Persian Period 549–332 B.C.

539 B.C. Cyrus, Persian conqueror of the Babylonian Empire, allows Jews to return to Jerusalem.

Greek Period 332–167 B.C.

334 B.C. Conquest by Alexander the Great. Palestine is controlled by the Ptolemies of Egypt.

198 B.C. Antiochus III of Syria defeats the Egyptians at Paneas (Caesarea Philippi) and Palestine is passed into the hands of the Seleucides.

175 B.C. Antiochus IV ("Epiphanes") becomes king. Abolishes worship of Jehovah; installs statue of the Olympian Zeus in the temple as the object of worship; offers swine on the temple altar.

Hasmonean Period 166–63 B.C.

Jewish revolt against the Seleucides led by an aged priest, Mattathias, and his sons Judas Maccabaeus ("The Hammer"), Jonathan, Simon, and their successors.

Roman Period 63 B.C.–A.D. 330

63 B.C. Roman conquest of Palestine by Pompey.

40 B.C. Parthians surprise Romans and take the land.

39 B.C. Herod the Great expells the Parthians and reigns until 4 B.C.

36–26 B.C. Pontius Pilate is procurator of Judea.

A.D. 30 Crucifixion of Jesus

A.D. 66 First Jewish revolt under the Zealots.

A.D. 70 Jerusalem is destroyed by Titus, son of Vespasian.

A.D.132–135 Second Jewish revolt under leadership of Bar-Kokhba. Hadrian rebuilds Jerusalem as a Roman city; calls it Aelia Capitolina. Under penalty of death, no Jew was to approach its environs. He also changes name of country from Judea to Syria Palestina (Syria of the Philistines); hence the name "Palestine."

Byzantine Period (Roman) A.D. 330–634

Constantinople (called Byzantium) is made capital of the eastern half of the Roman Empire. Christianity spreads rapidly after conversion of Emperor Constantine. Churches are built and Palestine flourishes.

Second Persian Period A.D. 607–629

A.D. 614 Jerusalem taken; 33,877 slain. Christian churches destroyed. The work of 300 years' construction obliterated.

Arab Period A.D. 634–1099

A.D. 570 Muhammad is born in Mecca. At age 43 he receives a series of revelations later gathered and published as the Koran. Dies in 632 but the faith of Islam has by then welded together the Arab tribes.

A.D. 636 All Palestine under Arab control. Jerusalem becomes Islam's third sacred city (the others are Mecca and Medina).

A.D. 1009 Fatimid Calif Hakim orders destruction of Church of the Holy Sepulchre. A reported 30,000 Christian buildings destroyed in Asia Minor. These atrocities spark the Crusades.

Crusader Period A.D. 1099–1263

A.D. 1098–99 First Crusade.

A.D. 1099 Jerusalem is taken by Crusaders and Latin Kingdom of Jerusalem is formed.

A.D. 1187 Saladin, a Muslim prince from Egypt, gains control of Egypt, Syria, and Mesopotamia and then unitedly marches on Palestine. The Crusaders are routed at the Horns of Hattin in Galilee. Jerusalem capitulates in 1187. Crusaders control Jerusalem for a short time in 1229 and in 1241. Mongol tribes from Central Asia take Jerusalem with a terrible slaughter in early thirteenth century.

Mameluk Period A.D. 1263–1516

A.D. 1263 Mameluk Sultan Baybers of Egypt capture remaining Crusader strongholds. Hold coastal cities intermittently for next 250 years.

A.D. 1400 Another Mongol invasion under Tamerlane.

Turkish Period A.D. 1517–1917

A.D. 1517 Palestine conquered by the Turkish Ottoman Empire and held for 400 years.

A.D. 1799 Napoleon makes unsuccessful attempt to add Palestine to his empire. He captures Jaffa (Joppa), then marches on Acre, but because his navy has been defeated by the Ottomans and the British at the Battle of the Nile, the French are unable to land their seige guns and Napoleon retreats to Egypt.

A.D. 1917 Jerusalem taken by the Allies in World War I under General Allenby.

Modern Period 1917—

A.D. 1917 Balfour Declaration.

A.D. 1922 British Mandate over Palestine.

A.D. 1948 British Mandate ends.

May 14, 1948 Jewish National Council establishes the state of Israel. Jewish-Arab War.

July 18, 1948. The fighting officially ends. Palestine is partitioned between Israel and Jordan by the United Nations.

June 5, 1967 Sparked by Gamal Abdel Nasser's closing of the Gulf of Aqaba to Israeli shipping, war begins between Israel and the Arab nations. Six days later it concludes with Israel controlling the Sinai Peninsula, the Gaza Strip, the Kuneitra (Golan) sector of Syria, and the formerly Jordanian-controlled West Bank of the Jordan River, including the eastern sector of Jerusalem. The old and new cities of Jerusalem become one, and the Jews have access to the Wailing Wall (Western Wall) for the first time since 1948.

1969 Fighting breaks out along Suez Canal.

October 1973 Syrian and Egyptian forces attack Israeli positions in Golan and along the Suez Canal. Israel pushes Syrians back beyond 1967 cease-fire lines and re-crosses canal. Renewed efforts at peace follow.

March 5, 1974 By agreement, Israeli forces pull back from the canal and Egypt assumes control of both banks.

September 1975 Interim agreement provides for another Israeli withdrawal in the Sinai Peninsula.

September 1978 Sadat and Begin meet with President Jimmy Carter at Camp David. They sign a treaty that results in Israel beginning a withdrawal from the Sinai on May 25. (The last settlers left in April 1982.) The two countries open their border on May 29.

July 17, 1981 Prime Minister Begin orders bombing raid against PLO (Palestine Liberation Organization) headquarters in Beirut, killing 300 and injuring 700.

June 9, 1982 Israel invades Lebanon in retaliation for alleged PLO attack that critically wounded the Israeli ambassador to London a week earlier.

September 15, 1983 Begin resigns.

March 1984 Lebanon cancels a U.S. mediated accord with Israel. Signed in May of the previous year, the accord would have provided for Israeli withdrawal from Lebanon, and gradual normalization of relations between the two countries.

September 14, 1984 National unity government—including both the Labor Alignment and the Likud bloc—is approved.

Places of Interest

Absalom's Pillar—On the east slope of the Kidron Valley, just opposite the southern portion of the temple area, is a prominent stone pillar known as Absalom's Pillar. Sometimes it is referred to as Absalom's Tomb, but his body is probably not buried there. This may be the pillar spoken of in 2 Samuel 18:17, 18. Adjacent to this pillar are sepulchres believed to be the tombs of St. James, Zachariah (father of John the Baptist), and Jehoshaphat. It was customary for the Jews to whitewash their tombs each year and it has been suggested that Jesus was referring to these very tombs in the Valley of Kidron when he accused the hypocritical Pharisees of being like whited sepulchres—beautiful on the outside but inside full of dead men's bones (Matt. 23:27).

Aceldama—On the southern side of the Valley of Hinnom, where it meets the Kidron Valley at the foot of the hill

Ophel, is the **Potter's Field,** called Aceldama ("The Field of Blood"). This is the field of which Zechariah prophesied (11:12, 13). It was purchased by the high priests with the thirty pieces of silver Judas threw down in the Temple after he realized the enormity of his crime of betraying Jesus (Matt. 27:3–10; Acts 1:18, 19). The field was to be a place in which to bury strangers.

Acre—Known by several names, Acre is one of the oldest cities in the world. It was known in the Old Testament times as **Accho** (Judg. 1:31). Located nine miles north of Haifa, it was assigned to the tribe of Asher but was not taken by them at that time (Josh. 19:24–31; Judg. 1:31). It was later called **Ptolemais** after the Ptolemies of Egypt. Paul stopped here briefly on his final trip to Jerusalem (Acts 21:7). It was a most important port because of an excellent harbor and ease of access to the interior by way of the Plain of Esdraelon, to the east, and to the north via the narrow pass, the Ladder of Tyre. During the Crusades Acre was their capital for more than one hundred years. The city is famous for the remains of Crusader construction as well as that of the Turks. It was the last place held by the Crusaders in Palestine, being taken from them by the Saracens in 1291. Napoleon's unsuccessful attempt to capture Acre, after a two-month seige in 1799, marked the end of his dream of an Eastern Empire. The town is now known as **Akko.**

Antipatris—North of Lydda (Lod) on the fertile plain of Sharon is the town called Antipatris. It is mentioned in Acts 23:31 as the place where soldiers taking Paul from Jerusalem to Caesarea stopped for the night. It was built around 35 B.C. by Herod and named after his father, Antipater. There is some reason for believing it was built on the site of ancient **Aphek,** mentioned as the place of battle to which Israel brought the ark of God from Shiloh and where it was captured by the Philistines (1 Sam. 4:1–11).

Arad—The new city of Arad, built near the site of the ancient city 17 miles south of Hebron, is the tenth to be built here. It is mentioned in the earliest accounts of the efforts of the children of Israel to penetrate the Promised Land from the south. The men of Arad took some of the children of Israel prisoners and Israel vowed to destroy this and other cities associated with them (Num. 21:1, 2; 33:40; Josh. 12:14; Judg. 1:16).

Ashdod—First mentioned as one of the homes of the giant Anakims (Josh. 11:22), Ashdod was one of the five great cities of the Philistines. It was included in the portion of land given to Judah but not occupied by that tribe until the time of Uzziah (2 Chron. 26:6; Josh. 13:3; 15:46–47).

Ashdod was the home of a temple built in honor of the Philistine god Dagon, and it was the first city to which the Philistines brought the ark of God after they had taken it from Israel. The next morning the image of Dagon was found fallen on its face before the ark (1 Sam. 5:1–7).

Several prophets prophesied against Ashdod for its enmity to Israel (Amos 1:8; Zeph. 2:4). These calamities were fulfilled when Sargon and the Assyrians took the city (Isa. 20:1). Nehemiah sternly rebuked the Jews who had intermarried with the women of Ashdod (Neh. 13:23–27).

The ancient city of Ashdod was located about 3 miles south of the present city of the same name. After Philip left the revival at Samaria to minister to the Ethiopian eunuch, he was found at **Azotus**—a place believed to be the same as ancient Ashdod (Acts 8:26–40).

Ashkelon—Ashkelon was one of the five most important Philistine cities (the other four being Gaza, Ekron, Ashdod, and Gath). It was the only one built on the coast with a harbor and was mentioned by Joshua (Josh. 13:3) and taken by the tribe of Judah (Judg. 1:18).

Here Samson slew thirty men and took their clothes and

possessions to pay off those who had discovered his riddle (Judg. 14:19). When King Saul was killed, David cried, "Tell it not in Gath, publish it not in the streets of Askelon; lest the daughters of the Philistines rejoice, lest the daughters of the uncircumcised triumph" (2 Sam. 1:20). The Philistines were among Israel's fiercest enemies and several of the prophets spoke against their cities, Ashkelon included (Jer. 25:20; 47:6, 7; Amos 1:8; Zeph. 2:4, 7). In relation to this last reference it is interesting to note that the main thoroughfare in modern Ashkelon is named Zephaniah Boulevard. The city is believed to be the birthplace of Herod the Great.

Beersheba—Beer-shev'a—It is interesting to note that Beersheba, in the days of the patriarchs (Abraham, Isaac, and Jacob) was neither a city nor a fortress. It was simply a cluster of wells in the open desert. It means "Well of the Oath" (Gen. 21:27–31). It probably served as a small wayside station for caravans traveling between Canaan and Egypt and the Arabian Peninsula.

Excavations have revealed that as far back as 5,000 years ago people lived in the area in underground villages. Subterranean homes have been found complete with furniture and domestic appurtenances.

After the days of Abraham it became a village of some size. However, at the beginning of this century there was nothing there, the site having been abandoned hundreds of years before. The Turkish rulers built a small administrative and marketing center for the Bedouin near the spot where the ancient city stood.

In 1917, during the First World War, Beersheba was the first town to be captured from the Turks by General Allenby. It was a wind-swept desert village of barely 2,000 population. When it fell to the Israeli Army in 1948 it numbered only about 3,000. Today, as a result of the efforts and energy of the nation of Israel, its population has multiplied many times and it is the capital of the Negev from which the entire southern part of the country is administered.

Beersheba was the southernmost city of Israel in Old Testament times, while Dan was the most northern (hence the frequently found expression, "from Dan even to Beersheba"—Judg. 20:1; 1 Sam. 3:20, etc.). Abraham lived for some time at Beersheba (Gen. 22:19); it was here he met Abimelech, king of the Philistines, and they made a covenant together (Gen. 21:22–34). Later Abraham's son Isaac dwelt here and built an altar to God; he also dug a well and made a covenant with the king of the Philistines (Gen. 26:23–33).

The Lord appeared to Hagar in the wilderness of Beersheba after she had been sent from Abraham's home (Gen. 21:9–20). From Beersheba Jacob began his journey to Haran in flight from the anger of his brother Esau (Gen. 28:10). Jacob stopped and offered sacrifices to God at Beersheba on his journey into Egypt to live with Joseph during the great seven-year famine (Gen. 46:1–5). Beersheba was part of the inheritance of the tribe of Simeon within the portion allotted to Judah (Josh. 19:1, 2). It was in this vicinity that Elijah, during his flight from the threats of Jezebel, sat under the juniper tree and wished he might die. Here the angel of the Lord served him the food, in the strength of which he went forty days and nights to Mount Horeb (1 Kings 19:1–8). Samuel's two unworthy sons were judges at Beersheba (1 Sam. 8:1–3).

Bethany—The village of Bethany is located 15 furlongs (1¾ miles) from Jerusalem on the eastern slope of the Mount of Olives; it is on the road to Jericho. Here was the home of Mary, Martha, and Lazarus (John 11:1), as well as that of Simon the leper (Mark 14:3). Jesus seemed to have made Bethany his home in Judea as he did Capernaum in Galilee (Matt. 21:17; Mark 11:11). No doubt this was because of the love he had for Mary, Martha, and Lazarus (John 11:5).

It was undoubtedly in Bethany that Mary sat at Jesus' feet while Martha was "cumbered about much serving" (Luke 10:38–42). Here occurred the great miracle of the raising of Lazarus from the dead after he had laid in the grave four days (John 11:1–44). It was at supper in the house of Simon the leper that Mary anointed Jesus with the precious spikenard and Judas complained of the waste of such costly ointment (Matt. 26:6–13; Mark 14:3–9; John 12:1–8).

From the vicinity of Bethany Jesus sent two of his disciples to get the donkey on which he rode into Jerusalem on Palm Sunday (Mark 11:1–11; Luke 19:29–40). While returning to Jerusalem from Bethany one morning Jesus cursed the barren fig tree (Mark 11:12–14; Matt. 21:17–22).

Christ's ascension from the Mount of Olives must have been close to the village of Bethany (Luke 24:50, 51).

Bethel—Located 11 miles north of Jerusalem, Bethel was one of the royal cities of the Canaanites (Josh. 12:16) and was allotted to Benjamin (Josh. 18:22), although it was the house of Joseph that took it from the Canaanites (Judg. 1:22–26). It was originally called **Luz** (Gen. 28:19).

It was here that Abraham built his second altar when he came into the land of Canaan from Ur of the Chaldees (Gen. 12:8). He returned here after the famine which took him into Egypt (Gen. 13:3, 4). Abraham and Lot then separated because of strife between their herdsmen (Gen. 13:5–12).

It was at Bethel ("The House of God") that Jacob spent the first night on his flight from the anger of his brother Esau (Gen. 28:11–22). On this night he saw the vision of the ladder set up on earth and the angels ascending and descending. When the Lord called Jacob back to Canaan, twenty years later, he spoke of Himself as "the God of Bethel" (Gen. 31:13), and it was to this spot Jacob returned with his family and his flocks (Gen. 35:1–15), at which time God renewed to Jacob the covenant concerning the land which he had previously made with Abraham and Isaac.

Samuel made a yearly circuit, in his ministry as judge and prophet, which included Bethel, Gilgal, and Mizpah (1 Sam. 7:16). It seemed to be an important center of worship (1 Sam. 10:3; see also 1 Kings 13).

At the time of the secession of the ten tribes and the

formation of the northern kingdom of Israel, Jeroboam was afraid the people would return their allegiance to Judah when they made the annual pilgrimage to Jerusalem at the feast time. To forestall this he made two golden calves and announced to the ten tribes, "Behold thy gods, O Israel, which brought thee up out of the land of Egypt." One of these was placed at Bethel, the other to the north in Dan. Priests were ordained and sacrifices made to these idols. This is the sin for which Jeroboam was known (1 Kings 12:26–33; note Jer. 48:13). Amos, the herdsman prophet, was forbidden by Jeroboam from prophesying in Bethel because he foretold the death of the king and the captivity of Israel (Amos 7:10–17). King Josiah destroyed this altar and high place and slew the priests who ministered there at the time of the great revival during his reign (2 Kings 23:4, 15–20).

Bethel was the first stop on Elijah's journey toward his translation. Elisha accompanied him (2 Kings 2:2, 3). On his return to Bethel from Elijah's translation Elisha was mocked by a group of little children, "Go up, thou bald head." He turned and cursed them in the name of the Lord and two she bears came and killed the children (2 Kings 2:23, 24).

Little may be seen in Bethel today in the way of archaeological findings because the excavations have been filled in so that the land may be used by the present inhabitants of the village.

Bethlehem—As the birthplace of Jesus, Bethlehem is one of the most picturesque and heart-touching places in the Holy Land. It lies about 5 miles south of Jerusalem and is built on the terraced hillside. It is first mentioned in the Bible as the place where Jacob's wife, Rachel, died while giving birth to Benjamin (Gen. 35:16–20; 48:7). Rachel's tomb is pointed out today just a little north of the city (note 1 Sam. 10:2). Ibzan, the tenth judge in Israel, was from Bethlehem (Judg. 12:8–10).

The beautiful story of the Book of Ruth centers in Bethlehem. It was from here Elimelech and Naomi went to Moab with their two sons at a time of famine (Ruth 1:1-2). After the death of her sons, Naomi, with Ruth her daughter-in-law, returned to Bethlehem (Ruth 1:19–22). Ruth married Boaz and became the great grandmother to David, king of Israel (Ruth 4:17; 2 Sam. 17:12). Thus Bethlehem is the original home of the Davidic family. This is the reason Joseph of Nazareth came here to pay his taxes (Luke 2:4–7), and thus it became the place where Jesus was born. The fields of Boaz where Ruth gleaned barley and wheat are still identified today.

It was at Bethlehem that Samuel the prophet anointed the boy David to be king of Israel in Saul's place (1 Sam. 16:4, 11–13). On the hills and fields of Bethlehem David tended his father's sheep (1 Sam. 17:15), and perhaps here experienced God's delivering power from the lion and the bear (1 Sam. 17:34–37).

The Philistines were occupying Bethlehem when David, becoming a little homesick, longed for a drink from the well of his boyhood town. Three of his mighty men broke through the ranks of the enemy and brought the water, but David refused to drink it, pouring it out as an offering to the Lord (2 Sam. 23:14–16; 1 Chron. 11:16–19).

Micah designated Bethlehem as the place where Israel's Messiah would be born (Mic. 5:2; Matt. 2:4–6; John 7:42). This prophecy was fulfilled in Luke 2:4–7. It was here the shepherds worshiped (Luke 2:15–16) and the wise men presented their gifts (Matt. 2:7–11). Herod the Great slew the innocent babes of Bethlehem endeavoring to destroy the one born King of the Jews (Matt. 2:16–18; Jer. 31:15).

The Church of the Nativity in Bethlehem is the oldest church in Christendom. Built over the cave where it is believed Jesus was born, the church was originally constructed by Constantine about A.D. 326. Marking the traditional birthplace is a silver star inscribed in Latin: "Here of the Virgin Mary, Christ was born."

Church of the Nativity, Bethlehem.

Bethphage—The site of Bethphage is on the slopes of the Mount of Olives between Bethany and the city of Jerusalem. It was from here the triumphal entry began (Matt. 21:1–11; Mark 11:1–11; Luke 19:29–40).

Bethsaida—Meaning "the place of catching," Bethsaida's name apparently refers to its association with the fishing industry. Peter, Andrew, and probably Philip, disciples of Christ, were fishermen from this village (John 1:44). The location of the city, called "Bethsaida Julius," was at the place where the Jordan River enters the Sea of Galilee. It was another community, along with Capernaum and Chorazin, that was spoken of by Jesus because of its unbelief and failure to repent (Matt. 11:21; Luke 10:13). No doubt it was because of the unrepentance of its inhabitants that Jesus took the blind man out of the city before He healed him (Mark 8:22–26). The "desert place" to which Jesus took His disciples after their first preaching experience, and where He fed the five thousand, was near Bethsaida (Luke 9:10). It is most significant that the three cities upon which the woes were pronounced are gone today, while Tiberias, which received no word of judgment from Jesus, is flourishing.

Beit-shean—About 17 miles due south of the Sea of Galilee is the city of Beit-shean, located where the Valley of Jezreel meets the Valley of the Jordan. It was inhabited as long ago as 3000 B.C. The Tell el-Hosn, as it is called, contains eighteen levels of ancient settlements. It was on the main caravan route from Egypt to Mesopotamia. Thus it often fell to rival armies who passed this way. Later it became a wealthy Greek center, the leading member of the Decapolis (the league of ten cities) and the only one west of the Jordan River. It declined under the Moslems and has remained no more than a village since then. The Jews are endeavoring to revive it now. It is called both **Beth-shan** and **Beth-shean** in the Bible. It was part of the inheritance of the tribe of Manasseh (Josh. 17:11), but the men of Manasseh were never able to subdue the Canaanites there (Judg. 1:27) because of their chariots of iron (Josh. 17:16). Beit-shean is at the foot of Mount Gilboa where Saul and Jonathan were slain. When their bodies were found the Philistines fastened them to the wall of Beth-shan. Valiant men from Jabesh-gilead came by night and took the bodies down from the wall and buried them (1 Sam. 31:8–13). These were later recovered by David and buried in the country of Benjamin (2 Sam. 21:12–14).

Archaeologic excavations have unearthed six temples, two of which date to the time of the Philistine rule and are believed to be those associated with the death of Saul.

Beth-shemesh—Beit-shemesh—About 20 miles west of Jerusalem are the excavated ruins of Beth-shemesh on a hill near Zorah where Samson was born (Judg. 13:2–25). It was to Beth-shemesh the Ark of the Covenant was borne by the two "milch kine" after it had brought so much distress to the Philistines during the seven months they kept it. The people of Beth-shemesh rejoiced when they saw the sacred ark coming and they offered the kine as a sacrifice unto the Lord. They made the serious mistake, however, of lifting the golden mercy seat and looking into the ark, thus exposing the two tables of the law. A great number of them were slain. The people of Beth-shemesh sent to Kirjath-jearim asking the men of that place to come and take the ark to their city (1 Sam. 6:7–21).

Bireh—Bireh is situated 15 miles north of Jerusalem, adjacent to the town of Ramallah. They virtually form one community. Bireh was the first stopping place for caravans going from Jerusalem to Galilee. It is therefore thought to be the place where Mary and Joseph first missed their son, Jesus, as they were returning from Jerusalem (Luke 2:41–45).

Caesarea—Located on the Mediterranean coast about midway between the city of Haifa and Tel Aviv is the city originally called "Strato's Tower" by the Phoenicians who built a small anchorage there about 250 B.C. The city of Caesarea itself was founded in 22 B.C. and built by Herod the Great. It was the capital of the Roman government in Palestine, named in honor of Caesar Augustus. Its palace, theater, hippodrome, aqueduct, and circular breakwater were famous. It is first mentioned in the New Testament as the northernmost city of Philip's evangelistic endeavors after his encounter with the Ethiopian eunuch (Acts 8:40).

Caesarea was the home of the godly centurion Cornelius, whose prayers resulted in the remarkable incidents surrounding Peter's vision on the housetop at Joppa, and in his being sent to preach the gospel in this Gentile's home (Acts 10:1–33). Here the opening of the door of the gospel to the Gentiles was manifest by the outpouring of the Holy Spirit as on the day of Pentecost (Acts 10:44–48).

Herod Agrippa I died at Caesarea, being "eaten of worms." He had just delivered such a notable speech that the people said, "It is the voice of a god, and not of man." Herod did not give God the glory and was smitten by the angel of the Lord (Acts 12:19–23).

Caesarea is mentioned on a number of occasions in relation to the experiences of the apostle Paul. He sailed from there to Tarsus after his first visit to Jerusalem following his conversion (Acts 9:30). Traveling from Ephesus to Jerusalem he stopped at Caesarea on the occasion described in Acts 18:22. When making his final journey to the holy city Paul and his company landed at Caesarea where he stayed a number of days in the house of Philip the evangelist, who was one of the seven chosen to oversee the ministry to the widows (Acts 6:3–6), and whom God used to bring the Gospel to the city of Samaria (Acts 8:5–8). While Paul was in Caesarea at this time, Agabus prophesied that if Paul went to Jerusalem he would be bound and delivered to the Gentiles. The apostle refused to be persuaded not to go (Acts 21:10–13).

After Paul was taken into custody in Jerusalem it was

discovered that forty men were determined to kill him, and he was taken by a group of soldiers to Caesarea (Acts 23:23–33). Three times he made his defense in outstanding addresses while there. The first was before Felix the governor of Judea, while Ananias the high priest and an orator named Tertullus accused him (Acts 24:1–22). After two years in Caesarea, during which Felix listened often to him (Acts 24:23–27), Paul was brought before the next governor, Festus, and was moved to appeal his case to Caesar (Acts 25:1–12). The third time Paul was allowed to speak in his own behalf while at Caesarea was before King Agrippa—Herod Agrippa II and brother-in-law to Felix (Acts 26).

The Great Jewish War, which ended four years later with the fall of Jerusalem, was begun by the Jews in Caesarea in A.D. 66. In the third century the celebrated Christian scholar Origenes established the school of Caesarea as a center of Christian learning. Eusebius was bishop of Caesarea and carried on the tradition of the school in the early part of the fourth century. Imposing Crusader fortifications were built here by Louis XIV of France in 1251. After these were captured by the Turks in 1265 the city was abandoned and buried by sand dunes.

Excavations and important findings at Caesarea have been quite extensive. These have uncovered the great aqueduct along the seashore which brought water to the city from the mountains some 12 miles away. The imposing ruins of the Crusader fortifications are very impressive as is the Roman theater, used now each year for musical productions. Here too, has been unearthed the first archaeological evidence of Pontius Pilate. It is an inscription bearing his name and the name of Emperor Tiberius.

Caesarea Philippi—At the base of Mount Hermon northeast of the Sea of Galilee is Caesarea Philippi, probably the northernmost point to which Jesus traveled. It was originally called Panias because it was the center of the pagan worship of the Greek fertility-god Pan. From a nearby cave (Mugharet

Ras en-Neba) flows a spring which is one of the principle sources of the Jordan River.

At the death of Herod the Great the region north and east of the Sea of Galilee was given to his son Philip. He rebuilt and enlarged the town and gave it the name of Caesarea in honor of the then-reigning emperor, Caesar Tiberius. The name Philippi was added to honor its builder, Philip, and to distinguish it from Caesarea on the coast midway between Haifa and the present city of Tel Aviv. The old name is still used with a slight variation—the town is now called **Banias.**

Mount Hermon, 9,101 feet above sea level, is by far the highest mountain in or near Palestine. It was sacred to the worshipers of the Canaanite deities and was the religious center of primeval Syria. Its Baal sanctuaries were well known before the exodus. It is mentioned in Joshua 11:17 and Joshua 12:1 and was sometimes called Baal-Hermon (Judg. 3:3).

Because of these close associations with pagan worship it is significant that Jesus should have chosen Caesarea Philippi as the place where he asked his disciples, "Whom do men say that I the Son of man am?" And here He elicited from Peter, through the revelation of the Father, the glorious confession, "Thou art the Christ, the Son of the living God." This was a great testimony in the heart of paganism (Matt. 16:13–16; Mark 8:27–30; Luke 9:18–21).

Because of its great height Mount Hermon, rather than Mount Tabor (1,850 feet high), is believed to be the "high mountain" where Jesus was transfigured before Peter, James, and John (Matt. 17:1; Mark 9:2; Luke 9:28). Mount Hermon's proximity to Caesarea Philippi and the fact that the account of the transfiguration follows Peter's great confession add to this theory, but no positive proof can be offered.

Cana—About 4 miles northeast of Nazareth on the road to Tiberias lies Cana, where Jesus performed his first miracle—the changing of water into wine at a wedding feast (John 2:1–11). A Franciscan church has been built upon the remains of what is believed to be the house where the miracle occurred. Stone waterpots, similar to those used in Christ's time, are shown. It was also at Cana that Jesus healed, from a distance, the nobleman's son in Capernaum (John 4:46–54). Cana was the home of Nathanael, one of the twelve disciples (John 21:2).

Capernaum—The city of Capernaum was located along the northwest shore of the Sea of Galilee, about 2½ miles from where the Jordan River enters that body of water. It was situated along the great trade route that went from Damascus to the Mediterranean coast and Egypt. Tolls were collected on this traffic by the Roman government and it was from the office of the Capernaum toll house that Jesus called Matthew (Levi) to be His disciple (Matt. 9:9; Mark 2:14; Luke 5:27–29). Here also Jesus paid tribute money with the coin Peter took from the fish's mouth (Matt. 17:24–27). Some have estimated that Capernaum, which was also an important military center (recall the Roman centurion who was stationed there), may have had as many as 10,000 inhabitants in Jesus' day. He made it his headquarters (Matt. 4:13–16) and it is called "His own city" (Matt. 9:1).

More of Christ's miracles were performed in Capernaum than in any other city. These include the healing of Peter's mother-in-law (Matt. 8:14–15; Mark 1:29, 31; Luke 4:38–39), the centurion's servant (Matt. 8:5–13; Luke 7:1–10), the palsied man let down through the roof (Matt. 9:1–8; Mark 2:1–12; Luke 5:18–26), the nobleman's son (John 4:46–54), the two blind men (Matt. 9:27–30), probably the healing of the woman with the issue of blood (Matt. 9:20–22; Mark 5:25–34; Luke 8:43–48), and the raising from the dead of the daughter of Jairus (Matt. 9:18–19, 23–26; Mark 5:21–24, 35–43; Luke 8:41–42, 49–56). The deliverance of the dumb demoniac (Matt. 9:32–34) took place here, as did the exorcism of the demoniac in the synagogue (Mark 1:21–27; Luke 4:31–36). In addition to these specific cases great multitudes were brought and were healed (Matt. 8:16–17). Christ's great discourse on the bread of life, as well as others, was delivered in Capernaum (John 6:24–71; Mark 9:33–50).

In spite of all these miracles Capernaum failed to repent of her sin and came under Christ's woes of judgment (Matt. 11:23–24; Luke 10:15). This judgment was fulfilled and Capernaum no longer exists. Excavations there have yielded ruins of one of the finest limestone synagogues in the Holy Land. Some have thought it might be the one built by the kindly centurion (Luke 7:1–5), and thus be the one in which Jesus preached; experts believe, though, that it was built in the second century A.D. However, there is every probability that it stands on the same spot as the original.

Carmel, Mount—A beautifully wooded mountain, Carmel extends in a rough triangular shape for about 15 miles in a southeasterly direction from the promontory which drops to the Mediterranean Sea near Haifa. In the language of Scripture it is often pictured as the symbol of beauty and fruitfulness, or majesty and prosperity (2 Chron. 26:10; Song of Sol. 7:5; Isa. 35:2; Jer. 46:18; 50:19). When Carmel is said to languish it is an indication of God's judgment upon the land (Nah. 1:4; Amos 1:2; Isa. 33:9).

From earliest times its heights were the site of altars to many strange gods. There are many remains of Canaanite shrines and caves where hermits found solitude. "Though they hide themselves in the top of Carmel," cried the prophet Amos, "I will search and take them out hence..." (Amos 9:3). An ancient altar to Jehovah also stood here (1 Kings 18:30). Thus it is not strange that Elijah should have chosen this place for the great contest with the prophets of Baal (1 Kings 18:19–39). The traditional site of this confrontation is where the Carmelite Monastery of St. Elijah now stands, about 500 feet above sea level. At the foot of the slope of Carmel, at the brook Kishon, Elijah slew all the prophets of Baal (1 Kings 18:40). On the top of Carmel, Elijah interceded until the three-and-one-half-year drought ended; from here he ran before the chariot of Ahab until he came to Jezreel, some 18 to 20 miles away (1 Kings 18:42–46). At the foot of Carmel in the "Cave of Elijah" is where that prophet is believed to have taken refuge on one of his flights from the anger of Ahab.

Chorazin—The ancient site of Chorazin is two miles north of Capernaum. It was one of the cities against which Jesus pronounced judgment because it refused to repent in spite of his ministry (Matt. 11:21–23; Luke 10:13–15). Ruins of an old synagogue of the third or fourth century have been uncovered there. The stones and pillars were made of black volcanic basalt.

Dan—Dan is a very familiar name in the Old Testament in that it was the city which marks the northern limit of the land of Israel (Beersheba was its southern extremity). The expression "from Dan even to Beersheba" is used in many places (Judg. 20:1; 1 Sam. 3:20; etc.). It is at the foot of Mount Hermon near one of the sources of the Jordan River.

Dan is first mentioned in the Bible as the location to which Abraham and his servants pursued the army of Chedorlaomer, and the three kings associated with him, in order to rescue Lot and his family and goods. The battle was continued until Abraham gained victory at Hobah, north of Damascus (Gen. 14:14–16).

The city was originally a Phoenician city called **Laish** (Judg. 18:27–29); it was also called **Leshem** (Josh. 19:47). Apparently the tribe of Dan was not satisfied with the inheritance allotted to them in the province of Judea (Josh. 19:40–47), much of it being occupied by the Philistines. So they sent an army of 600 men to capture Laish, far to the north, which they rebuilt and called Dan. The eighteenth chapter of Judges tells the dramatic story of this invasion and the setting up of a graven image which the tribe worshiped instead of going to Shiloh where the tabernacle had been set up.

When Jeroboam and the ten tribes revolted from Rehoboam and the house of Judah, after the death of Solomon,

Jeroboam set up his own kingdom known as Israel (1 Kings 12:16–20; 2 Chron. 10:12–19). Being afraid that if his people returned to Jerusalem to worship at the great temple their hearts would return to Judah and they would rebel against him, Jeroboam set up two places where his people could worship. He made two golden calves, putting one in Bethel in the south and the other in Dan, the northern extremity. He told Israel, "Behold thy gods, O Israel, which brought thee out of the land of Egypt" (1 Kings 12:26–33). Thus the northern kingdom fell prey to idolatrous pollution, and Jeroboam's great sin in leading Israel astray was associated with his name forever. He is almost always referred to after this as "Jeroboam, the son of Nebat, who made Israel to sin" (1 Kings 22:52; 2 Kings 3:3; 2 Kings 10:29; etc.).

During the war between Asa, king of Judah, and Baasha, king of Israel, the former hired Benhadad, king of Syria, to assist him; Benhadad smote the city of Dan (1 Kings 15:16–20; 2 Chron. 16:1–4). It was regained by Jeroboam II (2 Kings 14:25) but shared Israel's fate at the hands of Tiglath-pileser, being carried captive to Assyria (2 Kings 15:29).

Dead Sea—The Dead Sea is formed by the waters of the Jordan River and other small streams. In the Bible it is known as the Salt Sea (Gen. 14:3; Num. 34:3, 12; Josh. 15:2, 5; 18:19), and the Sea of the Plain (Deut. 3:17; Josh. 3:16; 12:3). It is the only place in the world where you can fly in an airplane more than 1,000 feet below sea level, being 1,302 feet below the normal level of the world's seas and oceans. Near its northern end it is about 1,300 feet deep, making its bottom 2,600 feet below sea level. It is approximately 50 miles long and averages about 10 miles in width.

There is no outlet but upward, by means of evaporation— at an average rate of approximately seven million tons per day. Only fresh water escapes this way, so the salinity and mineral content of the water are constantly increasing. The water (27 percent mineral) is five times saltier than the ocean, which is only 5 percent solid material. Consequently it is impossible to sink in Dead Sea waters. It is estimated that the waters which are not only salty but bitter, contain about 45 billion tons of valuable chemicals: mainly sodium, chlorine, sulphur, potassium, calcium, magnesium, and bromine.

The cities of Sodom and Gomorrah are believed to have been toward the lower end of the Dead Sea, possibly on a shallow extension called "The Tongue."

Dothan—About 14 miles north of Sebastia is Dothan. Here Joseph found his brothers and their flocks when his father sent him to look for them. They cast him in a pit and then sold him to the Ishmaelites for twenty pieces of silver (Gen. 37:13–28).

Dothan (Dothain, Tell Dotha) was also the city where the Syrian army surrounded Elisha and his servant. When the servant was filled with fear the following morning, the prophet prayed "Lord, I pray thee, open his eyes that he may see" and he saw the mountain "full of horses and chariots of fire round about Elisha" (2 Kings 6:13–23).

'Ein Karem—In a beautiful valley just west of Jerusalem is 'Ein Karem. It is believed to be the "city of Judah" (Luke 1:39) where John the Baptist was born (Luke 1:57–80). The Church of the Visitation marks the traditional site of the home of Zechariah and Elizabeth where Mary visited her cousin (Luke 1:39–56).

Elah, Valley of—About 20 miles west and a short distance south of Jerusalem is the Valley of Elah where David killed Goliath, the Philistine giant (1 Sam. 17:1–52). The Philistines occupied the hills on one side, Saul and the army of Israel on the hills opposite.

Elath—At the head of the Gulf of Aqaba, an arm of the Red Sea, is modern Elath (also called Elat or Eilat). It is located on the western side of the gulf in Israel, while the town of Aqaba is on the eastern side of the head of the gulf in the kingdom of Jordan. Both of these communities are near the biblical site of Elath and **Ezion-geber,** a short distance to the north. These last two places are the route the children of Israel took on their journey from Egypt to Canaan (Deut. 2:8). It is also in this area that King Solomon, in the middle of the tenth century B.C., "made a navy of ships in Ezion-geber, which is beside Eloth, on the shore of the Red sea, in the land of Edom" (1 Kings 9:26). This is the part of the country which certainly fulfills the prediction made to Israel that the Promised Land was "a land whose stones are iron, and out of whose hills thou mayest dig brass (copper)" (Deut. 8:9). Sixteen miles to the north lies Timna where a large new copper mining plant has been set up since Israel became a state in 1948. Here stand two russet-colored projections of rock called Solomon's Pillars.

Dr. Nelson Glueck, American archaeologist, made some astounding discoveries when he carried out an extensive excavation at Ezion-geber. He found that Solomon had done more than build a navy there. He had turned Ezion-geber into an industrial city with huge smelters and workshops. The smelters were ingeniously designed and located to take advantage of the constant north winds which blow off the gulf. These fanned the flames of the furnaces and kept them blazing at maximum heat all the time. According to Glueck, "No hand-bellows system was necessary, because with brilliant calculation, Solomon's engineers had harnessed the winds to furnish natural draught. The Bessemer principle of forced-air draught, discovered less than a century ago, was, in essence, already familiar three millenia back." The mines, furnaces, slag heaps, and the ruins of the enclosure Solomon built to keep his slave labor from escaping, are visible today.

Emmaus—Emmaus is the village toward which Cleopas and another disciple were walking when Jesus joined them after his resurrection. He talked with them and opened to them the Scriptures though they did not know him. He accepted their invitation to dine with them, and as he broke the bread their eyes were opened and they recognized him; he then vanished from their sight (Luke 24:13–35). Luke says that Emmaus was "from Jerusalem about three-score furlongs"—about 7½ miles.

Three villages are pointed out as the most probable locations of ancient Emmaus. One is Qubeibeh about 7 miles west of Jerusalem. Another is Amwas, about 20 miles west of Jerusalem, indicated by the writings of Eusebius and Jerome. Obviously the distance does not fit Luke's account, though much Roman Catholic tradition supports it. Third, the Crusaders believed that Emmaus was where the Arab village of Abu Ghosh now stands.

Endor—On the north side of the Valley of Jezreel (Esdraelon) near Mount Tabor is the city of Endor ('Ein-Dor) the dwelling place of the witch to whom Saul went on the eve of his final battle with the Philistines (1 Sam. 28:7–25). It is also mentioned as the place where some of Sisera's army perished (Ps. 83:9, 10).

En-gedi—Situated on the west shore of the Dead Sea about midway between its north and south ends, En-gedi is about 10½ miles north of Masada. In Bible days it was also known as Hazazon-tamar (2 Chron. 20:2) and was one of the cities in the inheritance of Judah (Josh. 15:62). The precipitous cliffs rise some 2,000 feet and are filled with caves; in these David and his men took refuge from King Saul (2 Sam. 23:29). Here also David spared Saul's life after cutting off part of his garments while he slept (1 Sam. 24). En-gedi ('Ein-Gedi) was famous for its verdure and fruitful vineyards made possible by immense springs of water which come out of the limestone cliffs. The fruitfulness of the area is extolled in the Song of Solomon (1:14). Ezekiel's prophecy (Ezek. 47:9, 10) looks forward to a time when the waters of the Dead Sea—like the river that flows into it—will be fresh enough for fish to exist in.

Esdraelon, Plain of—This, the largest valley in Israel, separates Galilee in the north from Samaria in the south. Throughout history, it has been a land bridge over which invading armies have marched while engaged in their many wars. The Pharaohs of Egypt, the Hittites, Israelites, Philistines, Assyrians, Syrians, Persians, Greeks, Romans, Crusaders, Turks, and even the British under Lord Allenby during World War I have marched and fought on the Plain of Esdraelon. John speaks of it as the site of the battle of Armageddon, the last great battle of this age (Rev. 16:13–16).

The Plain of Esdraelon is also referred to as the **Valley of Jezreel.** This expression is used more commonly in the Bible of the valley running eastward between Mount Gilboa and the Hill of Moreh, now known as **Giv'at Hamore.** In this valley Gideon and his three hundred soldiers routed the hosts of the Midianites (Judg. 6:33; 7). Here also, near where the archaeological site Tel Megiddo now stands, Sisera and his army were defeated by Israel under the leadership of Deborah and Barak (Judg. 4). Down this valley Elijah ran before the chariot of Ahab (1 Kings 18:46).

In spite of the tragedy and judgment that came upon Israel in the Valley of Jezreel, the prophet Hosea prophesies great blessing upon the nation in this very place (Hos. 1:10–11). This probably looks forward to their millennial blessing after the battle of Armageddon (Hos. 2:21–23).

Galilee, Sea of—Perhaps the supreme adventure in any visit to the Holy Land is to be at the Sea of Galilee. The ancient rabbis used to say that "Jehovah hath created seven seas, but the Sea of Galilee is His delight." Josephus called it "The Ambition of Nature."

This beautiful body of water, which played such an important role in the ministry of our Lord, is known by five different designations. In the Old Testament it is called "the sea of Chinnereth" (Num. 34:11; Josh. 12:3; 13:27, etc.). The modern name, **Lake Kinneret,** is the same, meaning "harp" (possibly because the lake is shaped like a harp). Later it was called "the lake of Gennesaret" (Luke 5:1) from the fertile plain on its northwest shore. When Herod Antipas built Tiberias and made it his capital, the lake became known as "the Sea of Tiberias" (John 6:1, 23; 21:1). The name by which it is best known is "Sea of Galilee" (Matt. 4:18; 15:29; Mark 1:16; 7:31; John 6:1). It is 13 miles long and about 7½ miles wide at its northern end and 32 miles in circumference. It lies almost 700 feet below sea level and its greatest depth is 200 feet. The lake abounds in fish as it must have in Christ's day. On its north shore Jesus called Peter, Andrew, James, and John—fishermen by trade (Matt. 4:18–22).

In Jesus' day the west shore from Tiberias to the Jordan River at the north end must have been an almost continuous series of cities. Actually there were nine of them. Today only Tiberias remains. Magdala (Matt. 15:39), the home of Mary Magdalene (Luke 8:2; Mark 16:9), was situated three miles north of Tiberias. Just beyond Magdala is the Plain of Gennesaret (Matt. 14:34; Mark 6:53), one of the most fertile areas of this part of the country.

North of Magdala, before Capernaum, is Tabgha and its Church of the Multiplication. This was built to mark the place of the miracle of the feeding of the five thousand (Matt. 14:13–21; Mark 6:32–44; Luke 9:10–17; John 6:1–14). However, this miracle probably took place on the opposite side of the Sea of Galilee in the wilderness near Bethsaida; thus the church of Tabgha merely commemorates this event.

Above the Plain of Gennesaret rises the Mount of the Beatitudes where it is believed Jesus spoke those wonderful principles of the blessed life (Matt. 5:1–12) and the Sermon on the Mount (Matt. 5–7). In one of the sheltered coves, which form a natural amphitheatre, Jesus borrowed Peter's boat and from it spoke to the multitude (Luke 5:1–3).

Galilee yielded two remarkable catches of fish in response to Jesus' commands (Luke 5:4–11; John 21:6–8). Sudden and violent storms often rush down on the lake from the high peaks of Hermon and the Lebanon Mountains not far to the north. Two of these storms revealed the omnipotence of Jesus, even over the powers of nature. In one storm he was in a boat with the disciples (Matt. 8:23–27; Mark 4:35–41; Luke 8:22–25); in the other he came walking on the stormy water to the disciples in a boat (Matt. 14:22–33; Mark 6:45–52; John 6:15–21).

On the eastern side of the lake the cliffs rise as much as 2,000 feet above the shore. Down one of these cliffs the two thousand head of swine plunged into the sea after Jesus had cast the demons out of the demoniac and permitted them to enter the herd of swine (Matt. 8:28–34; Mark 5:1–21; Luke 8:26–40).

Before His crucifixion Jesus promised his disciples he would meet them in Galilee following his resurrection (Mark 14:28). Reiterated by the angel of the tomb (Mark 16:7), this was fulfilled at the early morning breakfast meeting by the shore of Galilee (John 21).

Gaza—Gaza is situated about 40 miles south of Jaffa (Joppa). It was one of the five principle cities of the Philistines and probably the oldest. It has always been important for it lies at the southern end of the Fertile Crescent joining Assyria and Egypt. It has been conquered by every world power which has held sway in the Middle East.

Joshua reached Gaza (Josh. 10:41) but it is doubtful if he ever conquered it (Josh. 11:22). The tribe of Judah captured the city (Judg. 1:18) but probably did not hold it long for it was a Philistine city in the days of Samson, whose exploits have made it famous. To escape being killed by the Philistines, Samson carried off the gates of the city on his shoulders and deposited them in Hebron about 40 miles away (Judg. 16:1–3). It was to Gaza that Samson was taken after the Philistines had captured him following his seduction by Delilah. The Philistines put out his eyes and made him grind in the prison house (Judg. 16:21). He met his death in Gaza when he pulled down the pillars of the house of Dagon, taking three thousand Philistines to death with him (Judg. 16:23–30).

Several of the Hebrew prophets spoke against Gaza (Amos 1:7; Zeph. 2:4). It is only mentioned once in the New Testament, when Philip was directed by the angel of the Lord to go from Jerusalem to Gaza, where he met and baptized the Ethiopian eunuch (Acts 8:26).

Geba—Geba was a town on the border of the inheritance of the tribe of Benjamin (Josh. 18:24), 6 miles north of Jerusalem, across the valley to the south from Michmash. It was one of the cities given to the Levites (Josh. 21:17; 1 Chron. 6:60). Its modern name is **Jeba.** It was on the northern boundary of the kingdom of Judah. The expression, "from Geba to Beersheba," marked the whole extent of the kingdom of Judah (2 Kings 23:8).

In the second year of his reign King Saul undertook to drive the Philistines from his realm. Jonathan, his son, struck the first blow at Geba (1 Sam. 13:3). This was followed up by Jonathan and his armorbearer's almost impossible feat as they climbed up the rocky gorge toward Michmash and smote the Philistines. This, certainly with the help of the Lord, put the enemy to confusion and flight (1 Sam. 14:1–23).

Geba was among the cities reoccupied by Judah after the 70-year exile in Babylon (Ezra 2:26; Neh. 11:31).

Gerar—Gerar was an ancient Philistine city on the border between Palestine and Egypt (Gen. 10:19). It seems definitely to be associated with Tell el-Jemmel, which has been partly excavated by Sir Flinders Petrie. It is located 8 miles southeast of Gaza on the way to Beersheba.

It was at Gerar that Abraham repeated his act of calling Sarah his sister rather than his wife (Gen. 12:11–20; Gen. 20). Only God's intervention in each of these instances hindered disgrace to Sarah and confusion with regard to God's plans concerning Abraham's seed. Strangely enough, Isaac repeated his father's folly at the same place many years later (Gen. 26:6–11). Excavations lead us to believe that Gerar controlled a rich caravan trade in spices and incense between Arabia and Palestine and the West.

Gethsemane, Garden of—Gethsemane probably means "oil press." John (18:1) speaks of it as a garden across the Kidron from Jerusalem, and Luke (22:39) tells us it was on Olivet, which was across the Kidron from the Golden Gate of Jerusalem. It was a place where Jesus often went to pray (Luke 22:39). Judas seemed to know where he could find Jesus to betray him to the priests in the absence of the populace (Luke 22:6). It was the place of Jesus' agony, his betrayal, and arrest (Matt. 26:36–56; Mark 14:32–52; Luke 22:39–53; John 18:1–14).

The original area of Gethsemane must have been much larger than it is now for Jesus and his disciples to have found solitude there. The present garden is maintained by the Franciscans, and contains eight ancient olive trees. It is doubtful if these are the same trees which were there in the time of Christ, for Josephus tells us Titus cut down all the trees in the environs of Jerusalem during his siege of the city in A.D. 70. Because of the nature of olive trees it is possible that these eight may have grown from the roots of those under which Jesus prayed on that memorable night.

Adjacent to the Garden is the Church of All Nations in which is said to be the very rock by which Jesus prayed. The church is so named because sixteen nations contributed to its construction: Argentina, Australia, Belgium, Brazil, Britain, Canada, Chile, France, Germany, Hungary, Ireland, Italy, Mexico, Poland, Spain, and the United States.

Gibeah—Gabbath—In the hill country, about 4 miles north of Jerusalem, and east of the road to Ramallah is the site of king Saul's hometown, sometimes called in the Bible Gibeah of Benjamin and sometimes Gibeah of Saul (1 Sam. 11:4; 13:16; 15:34). It is now known as **Tel el-Ful.** Excavations point to four great fortresses having been built one on another. The first points back to the destruction by fire referred to in Judges 20:40. On the ruins of this was built what was probably the fortress of Saul's time. Its remains measure 170 by 155 feet and its sloping walls were 6 feet thick. Later two other smaller fortresses were built on top of these.

The sordid story of the abuse heaped upon the Levite and his concubine, which led to the civil war that almost exterminated the tribe of Benjamin, took place at Gibeah (Judg. 19:12–30; 20:1–48).

After Saul had been crowned as the first king of Israel, he returned to his home in Gibeah accompanied by a "band of men whose hearts God had touched" (1 Sam. 10:26). It was from here Saul came to the aid of the men of Jabesh-gilead in their conflict with Nabash and the Ammonites (1 Sam. 11:4ff.) Saul and Jonathan made Gibeah the headquarters of their army in the battle with the Philistines described in First Samuel 13 and 14. It was at Gibeah of Saul that the bodies of the seven sons of Saul were hung up by the men of Gibeon (2 Sam. 21:6–9) because Saul had transgressed the covenant made with them by Joshua (Josh. 9:15).

Gibeon—About 8 miles northwest of Jerusalem is the village of **El-Jib,** which has been identified as Gibeon where the sun stood still in the days of Joshua (Josh. 10:12–13). The inhabitants of Gibeon, hearing what Israel had done to Jericho and Ai, had tricked Joshua into making a league with them (Josh. 9:3–27). When they heard of this covenant, five kings of the Amorites joined together to fight against Gibeon. The Gibeonites immediately called to Joshua for help. He marched all night to come to their aid and in the great battle which ensued God sent hailstones from heaven destroying more of the enemy than the Israelites killed. In order to finish the destruction of the enemy and not to be hampered by darkness, Joshua commanded the sun and moon to stand still at Gibeon and in the nearby Valley of Ajalon. The five defeated kings hid in a cave at Makkedah near Azekah and were subsequently slain by Joshua (Josh. 10:1–27). Gibeon was the only city that made peace with the Israelites in their conquest of Canaan, and they were made servants to Israel (Josh 11:19). Gibeon became part of the territory of the tribe of Benjamin and was given to the Levites as one of their cities (Josh. 21:17). Gibeon on one spectacular occasion was called Helkath-hazzurim, "The Field of Swords."

There is a great pool here at which an unusual contest of arms probably took place. As recounted in 2 Samuel 2:12–16, an attempt was made to settle a quarrel between the army of Ishbosheth, under Abner, and of David, under Joab, by having twelve men from each side fight. The plan failed because the twenty-four killed each other.

The pool in the story is part of Gibeon's spectacular water system. Cut entirely from solid rock, it includes the pool, 82 feet deep, 37 feet in diameter, and equipped with a circular stairway of 79 steps. Beyond the pool there is a tunnel, again carved from solid rock a distance of 167 feet, leading to a spring outside the ancient city.

King Saul failed to honor the ancient covenant with the Gibeonites and slew a number of them. Later, during the reign of David, the Lord sent a three-year famine on Israel as a judgment for Saul's deeds. The Gibeonites refused to accept a settlement of silver or gold and were only appeased when they had hanged seven of Saul's sons whom they had insisted should be delivered to them (2 Sam. 21:1–9).

When David brought the ark of God back to Jerusalem (2 Sam. 6:12; 1 Chron. 15:1, 25–29), it seems that the tabernacle of the congregation was situated at Gibeon (2 Chron. 1:3–6). Here Solomon offered one thousand burnt offerings. That night, in a vision, he was given a choice of anything he might ask of God. He prayed for a wise and understanding heart to enable him to govern Israel. God was pleased with such a request and promised Solomon riches as well (1 Kings 3:4–15; 2 Chron. 1:2–17).

Gilboa, Mount—Rising on the eastern edge of the Plain of Esdraelon is Mount Gilboa, the site of the defeat and death of Saul and his sons Jonathan, Abinadab, and Melchishua (1 Sam. 28:4; 1 Sam. 31:1–6; 2 Sam. 1:5–10; 2 Chron. 10:1–7). The death of Saul and Jonathan called forth the eloquent and heart-rending lament from David, wherein he prays that no dew will ever fall again on Mount Gilboa (2 Sam. 1:19–27). The River Kishon takes its rise on the slopes of Mount Gilboa.

Harod, Well of—At the foot of Mount Gilboa is the spring at which Gideon gathered the people of Israel to fight against Midian (Judg. 7:1). Here, at the Well of Harod ('Ein Harod), the diminished host of ten thousand was made to drink, and God chose to deliver the Midianites into the hands of the three hundred who lapped the water (Judg. 7:4–7).

Hazor—Hazor, a city of importance in earliest ages, is located ten miles north of the Sea of Galilee. It is mentioned as early as the nineteenth century B.C. in documents from Egypt. The first city was built more than 4,500 years ago. In the eighteenth century B.C. it was the largest city in the country and one of the largest in the Middle East. It was a frequent point of attack and was destroyed and rebuilt on a number of occasions through the centuries.

When Joshua and the children of Israel invaded the country, Jabin, king of Hazor, gathered together all the kings of that region to fight against them. God encouraged Joshua, and Israel won a great victory over this combined might. He took the city of Hazor and burned it to the ground (Josh. 11:1–13). When Israel did evil in the sight of the Lord after the death of Ehud, the second judge, "the Lord sold them into the hand of Jabin king of Canaan (Judg. 4:2). He apparently is a later Jabin who had recovered Hazor, for he was reigning there. He was noted for having nine hundred iron chariots and he held dominion over Israel for twenty years. The captain of his army was Sisera. Under the inspiration of Deborah, a prophetess, Barak led the children of Israel to a great victory over Sisera and his hosts in the Esdraelon Valley (Judg. 4:1–24).

Solomon, during his reign, rebuilt Hazor, Megiddo, and Gezer, three cities which dominated the plains of Huleh, Jezreel, and Ajalon, respectively (1 Kings 9:15). Hazor was conquered by the Assyrian king Tiglath Pileser in 732 B.C.

Hebron—Hebron lies about twenty miles in a southwesterly direction from Jerusalem. In ancient times it was known as Kirjath-arba (Josh. 14:15; 20:7). In Arabic, Hebron is called El Khalil ("the friend") after Abraham (2 Chron. 20:7; Isa. 41:8; James 2:23). After his separation from Lot, Abraham came and dwelt here, building his fourth altar "in the plain of Mamre, which is in Hebron" (Gen. 13:18). As a city, Hebron did not exist in Abraham's day, being founded about 1700 B.C. (Num. 13:22). The terraced hills were famous for their olive groves and fig trees. It was from this area that the spies took back to Kadesh Barnea "a branch with one cluster of grapes, and they bare it between two upon a staff" (Num. 13:22–23). This was the part of the country inhabited by the sons of Anak, the giants.

It was in this Hebron area that God appeared to Abraham in the form of three men and reconfirmed His promise of the birth of Isaac (Gen. 18:1–15). Here also Abraham made intercession for Sodom and Gomorrah (Gen. 18:16–33). The oak at Mamre, under which it is believed Abraham had pitched his tent, still exists. Its heavy branches are supported by steel beams and it is carefully surrounded by a high iron fence.

Abraham's wife, Sarah, died at Hebron and was buried in the cave of Machpelah, which Abraham purchased from the sons of Heth (Gen. 23). It was the only portion of Canaan that Abraham actually owned, though God had promised him the whole land. Later Abraham was buried beside

Sarah, as were Isaac, Rebecca, Jacob, and Leah, in the years that followed. A huge mosque is built over the cave; inside cenotaphs commemorate those who are buried below. A limited view of the cave may be had through a small opening, but no one is allowed to enter it. To the Moslems, Abraham was the first Moslem. Because of its association with Abraham, Hebron is regarded as one of the four sacred cities of Islam.

From Hebron Abraham went out to rescue Lot (Gen. 14:13–16). Isaac lived here for a time (Gen. 35:27). Jacob lived here after the death of Rachel (Gen. 37:14). Joseph traveled from Hebron to Dothan in search of his brothers and their sheep (Gen. 37:13–19).

Hebron was taken by Joshua in his conquest of the land of Canaan (Josh. 10:36–37) and was given to Caleb as his inheritance because of his faithfulness in following the Lord (Josh. 14:10–15). It was later designated one of the six cities of refuge (Josh. 20:7; 21:13).

At the gate of Hebron Joab treacherously killed Abner, who had been Saul's general, and paved the way for his master, David, to be king of all Israel (2 Sam. 3:27–39). After the death of Saul, David was crowned king of Judah at Hebron (2 Sam. 2:1–4). David reigned here seven and one-half years before he was made king of all Israel (2 Sam. 2:11; 1 Kings 2:11). Absalom, David's son, made Hebron his headquarters in his revolt against his father (2 Sam. 15:7–12).

The **Herodium**—A few miles southeast of Bethlehem stands an artificially heightened hill created by Herod the Great in a colossal earth-moving operation. Called the Herodium, it was built as both a place of retreat for Herod as well as another in a series of fortresses he built throughout the land (including the Alexandrium in the Jordan Valley and Masada). At its foot were palaces, terraced gardens, and pools; two hundred white marble steps led to towers of a citadel located on top. When Herod died in his summer palace at Jericho in 4 B.C. his body was taken to the Herodium which he had chosen as the place of his tomb. It is perhaps significant that his burial place was not far from Bethlehem, where he had ordered the slaying of the infants at the time of the birth of Jesus.

Hinnom, Valley of—West of Mount Zion and running around the southern side of the walled city of Jerusalem to the Kidron Valley, south of the hill Ophel, is the Valley of Hinnom. It is also called "valley of the son of Hinnom" (Josh. 15:8; 2 Chron. 28:3; 33:6; etc.) and "valley of the children of Hinnom" (2 Kings 23:10).

Located in this valley was Topheth, "the place of burning" (Jer. 7:31). During the reign of Ahaz and of Manasseh, idolatrous practices were carried on in this valley, including the offering of children as burnt sacrifices to abominable heathen gods (2 Chron. 28:3, 33:6). During his great revival, Josiah is said to have "defiled Topheth, which is in the valley of the children of Hinnom" that no more horrible sacrifices might be made there (2 Kings 23:10).

Because of the evil practices conducted in the valley, Jeremiah announced a change of its name to "the Valley of Slaughter" (Jer. 7:31–33). It became a place for burial until there was no more room and the bodies were just cast into it to be consumed by dogs and vultures. Fires were kept burning there continually to consume the rubbish of the city.

Jesus used the word "Gehenna"—taken from the Aramaic "Ge-Hinnom"—to signify eternal hell (Matt. 5:22, 29, 30; 10:28; 18:9; 23:15, 33; Mark 9:43, 45, 47; Luke 12:5; James 3:6).

Jenin—Thirteen miles north of Dothan is the town of Jenin—ancient En-gannim (Josh. 15:34; 19:21; 21:29). According to tradition, it was here that Jesus healed the ten lepers, only one of whom returned to give him thanks (Luke 17:11–19).

Jericho—Located in a very fertile plain north of the Dead Sea and west of the Jordan River is Jericho, also called "The City of Palm Trees" in the Bible (Deut. 34:3; 2 Chron. 28:15). Herod the Great built a luxurious palace here and made Jericho his winter capital. He died here in 4 B.C.

Jericho is specially known as the first city Joshua and the children of Israel took in their conquest of the land of Canaan. Here the spies were received and protected by Rahab (Josh. 2), and there the walls of the city fell down after the people of Israel had encircled them a total of thirteen times (Josh. 6). Joshua pronounced a curse against anyone who would attempt to rebuild the city (Josh. 6:26). First Kings 16:34 tells of one man who tried to do so and of the judgment he endured.

Jericho was one of the places to which Elisha followed Elijah on the journey that led to Elijah's translation (2 Kings 2:4–5). From the mound of ancient Jericho (known as **Tell es-Sultan**) one looks down on the Spring of Elisha whose waters were made sweet as the prophet put salt in them (2 Kings 2:18–22). The women still come with their waterpots, or modern five-gallon oil cans, to draw the family's supply of water.

Extensive excavations have been made at Jericho since early in the twentieth century. Claims have been made that the ruined walls of Joshua's time have been uncovered, but none of these are apparent today. This may be because some of the earliest archaeologists tore apart a section of the ancient city so that it is lost to scientific study. Other unearthed ruins have been destroyed by the elements. However, extensive ruins have been uncovered which date back to 7000 B.C. and earn for Jericho the distinction of being probably "the oldest walled city in the world." Outstanding is a huge defense system and an old tower thirty-five feet thick.

The modern city of Jericho is located to the east of the ancient site. It was outside modern Jericho that Jesus healed blind Bartimaeus (Mark 10:46–52; Luke 18:35–43). He also encountered Zacchaeus sitting in one of the sycamore trees that were abundant here (Luke 19:1–10). The road from Jericho to Jerusalem was the scene of Christ's story of the Good Samaritan (Luke 10:30–37).

West of Jericho, overlooking the Jordan valley, the hills of the western highlands rise abruptly. Just a mile from the city is the 1,500-foot-high ridge known as **Jebel Kuruntul.** Here the spies who were protected by Rahab hid for three days before returning to Joshua (Josh. 2:15–23). It is believed that this is the mountain to which the Holy Spirit led Jesus, immediately after His baptism in the Jordan, to be tempted of the devil. Here he fasted for forty days and nights and then triumphed over Satan with three simple but direct quotations from the book of Deuteronomy (Matt. 4:1–11; Mark 1:12–13; Luke 4:1–13).

Jerusalem—For the Christian, the most important place in the Holy Land is the city of Jerusalem—because of its place in antiquity, because of its association with the many vital events in the life of our Lord, and because of its future significance during the coming kingdom age.

The city of Jerusalem might well be called the world's most hated city, for though its name means "peace," more wars have been fought at its gates than at any other city in the world. But Jerusalem is also the world's most loved city for it is sacred to the three great religions of the world: Christianity, Mohammedanism, and Judaism. Pilgrims by the tens of thousands come each year to walk her streets and worship at her memorable places

Jerusalem is situated on a rocky prominence about 2,500 feet above the Mediterranean and 3,800 feet above the Dead Sea. It is 33 miles east of the Mediterranean Sea and 14 miles west of the Dead Sea.

The city's history goes back into the hazy past, at least to the fifteenth century B.C. It was called "Urusalimu" in Egyptian and Babylonish literature, hence its present name. Jerusalem is first mentioned in the Bible as Salem, which also means "peace" (Gen. 14:18). When the Israelites conquered Canaan, Jerusalem was known as Jebus and its inhabitants Jebusites (Judg. 19:10–11; 1 Chron. 11:4). The strong city which the Jebusites had built on the hill was considered impregnable, but David and his men took it against the taunts of the inhabitants (2 Sam. 5:6–9; 2 Chron. 11:4–7). David made Jerusalem his capital and brought the Ark of the Covenant there (2 Chron. 15).

The city which David captured was on the hill Ophel, south of the walls of the present city, with the Kidron Valley on the east and the Valley of Hinnom to the south. It was probably not more than 8 acres in size. Solomon built the beautiful temple on Mount Moriah immediately to the north.

Jerusalem has been captured twenty-six times in its history, and on at least five occasions has been totally destroyed. Nebuchadnezzar, king of Babylon, destroyed the city in 586 B.C. and carried the Jews into captivity (2 Kings 25:1–21; 2 Chron. 36:15–21; Jer. 39:9–14). Nehemiah rebuilt the walls after Cyrus, the Persian monarch, gave him permission (Ezra 1:1–11; 6:1–3; Neh. 2:4–20; 6:15–16). Other conquerors include Alexander the Great in 332 B.C. and Antiochus Ephiphanes in 168 B.C.

At the time of Jesus, the city had been greatly enlarged, particularly as the result of the building activities of Herod the Great. The city spread to the north and west of the original location on the hill Ophel. The present walls of the Old City were built in 1542 during the reign of the Turkish Sultan Suleiman—called "The Magnificent." In it there are eight gates and thirty-four towers. The modern city, capital of Israel, sprawls far beyond the walls to the northwest.

In accordance with the prophecy of Jesus (Luke 19:41–44; Luke 21:20–24), Jerusalem was destroyed in 70 A.D. by the Roman legions under Titus. At least nine times since then its control has passed from one religion to another. Emperor Hadrian built a pagan city on this site which he called Aelia

Walled City of Jerusalem

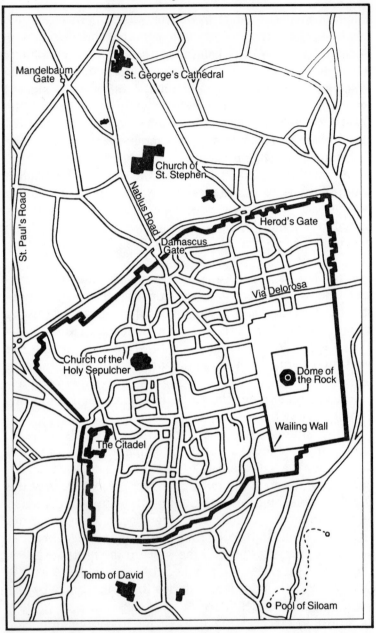

Map of the Old City. As of June 1967 there is no longer a No Man's Land separating this sector from modern Jerusalem.

Capitolina. Since then it has been held by Christians (third century), the Persians (seventh century), Arabs, the Crusaders, Arabs under Saladin, and the Ottoman Turks from A.D. 1517 until the Allied troops under Allenby entered its gates in 1917. After World War I Jerusalem and Palestine were placed under British Mandate. This was given up in 1948. The War of Liberation resulted in a United Nations Armistice, partitioning the city between Israel and Jordan. During the Six-Day war of 1967 Israel took the Old City and united Jerusalem with free access to each section for all.

Points of interest in Jerusalem center around:

Via Dolorosa—This is the traditional pathway Jesus took from Pilate's judgment hall to Calvary. It begins at the site of the Antonia, Herod's great fortress. It was here Paul made his speech to the people of Jerusalem (Acts 21:35–40). Here also was the tower of Hananeel in Nehemiah's day (Neh. 3:1; 12:39; Jer. 31:38; Zech. 14:10). The "Ecce Homo Arch" commemorates the words of Pilate: "Behold the Man" (John 19:5). Some feet below the present roadway, under the convent of the Sisters of Zion, can be seen the pavement upon which Jesus walked as he went out of the judgment hall (John 19:13). It is called the Lithostrotos (Hebrew *Gabbatha*).

Visitors are shown both the prison cell of Barabbas and the one occupied by Christ. The Church of the Holy Sepulchre has been built over what is believed to be the site of Calvary and the tomb of Joseph of Arimathaea. The church is a round building with the tomb in the center. Some distance away and 14 feet higher is a chapel built over what is thought to have been the hill of Calvary. There are three main shrines, plus many others split up between six churches: the Latin (Roman), Eastern Orthodox, Arminian, Coptic, Syrian, and Abyssinian.

Gordon's Calvary and the Garden Tomb, located outside the walls of the Old City, are held by many to be the true location of these sacred places. Whatever may be said for or against either location, the latter certainly gives one a clearer picture of what these places must have looked like in the time of our Lord.

Golden Gate—Also known as the Eastern Gate, Jerusalem's Golden Gate is on the east side of the city facing the Mount of Olives. This is the gate built on the place where it is believed Jesus entered on the occasion of his triumphal entry. It was closed by the Turkish governor of Jerusalem in 1530 in the hope of postponing the day of judgment and the end of the world. Legend had it that this would be the spot where the trumpet would sound and the dead would be raised. Many Christians believe that when Jesus comes again, the gate will be opened and he will once again enter the Holy City (Ezek. 44:1–3). If the gate were open it would be the only gate that would lead directly into the temple area.

St. Stephen's Gate—Also on the east side of the city, St. Stephen's Gate is the site of the martyrdom of Stephen while Saul of Tarsus was looking on (Acts 7:57–60). It is also called the Sheep Gate, and sometimes the Lions' Gate because of figures of lions on the gate.

The Dome of the Rock—To the left and to the south as one enters Jerusalem by St. Stephen's Gate is the great area surrounding Al-Haramesh-Sharif—the Dome of the Rock. This stands on what is believed to be Mount Moriah, where Abraham nearly offered Isaac as a sacrifice to God in obedience to the Lord's command (Gen. 22:1–2). This was also the threshing floor of Ornan the Jebusite (Araunah in Second Samuel) which David bought as a place of sacrifice to Jehovah that the plague might be stayed (2 Sam. 24:18–25; 1 Chron. 21:18–30). On this site Solomon built the first great temple (2 Chron. 3:1–2), later destroyed in 586 B.C. by Nebuchadnezzar (2 Kings 25:9; 2 Chron. 36:18–19). The second temple was built by Zerubbabel (Ezra 3:8–13; 4:23–24; 5:1–5; 6:15–18) and was rebuilt and enlarged by Herod the Great about 20 B.C.. This was the temple in existence in the time of Christ and to which his disciples called his attention in Matt. 24:1–2 (see also Mark 13:1–2; Luke 21:5–6).

The golden-domed, octagonal shaped mosque with its brilliant blue Persian tiles stands today where the Jewish temples formerly stood. The present building was erected in the last part of the seventh century over and around an immense, rough-hewn rock about 40 by 52 feet which rises 7 feet above the level of the temple area. It formed the base of the Jewish Altar of Burnt Offering. There are grooves in the rock, and a hole in the middle through which the blood and refuse were taken out of the temple and through the Dung Gate of the city to the valley below. It is from this area of the Dome of the Rock that Mohammed is supposed to have gone to heaven on his winged steed, el-Baruk ("Lightning"). The rock is considered second only in sanctity to Mecca and Medina as a Moslem shrine.

The Wailing Wall—A portion of the western wall of Herod's temple was preserved by the Romans when they destroyed the city in 70 A.D. to show how formidable they were. This fragment of wall is revered by the Jews and called The Wailing Wall. It is about 50 yards long and 60 feet high. Many of its stones measure 30 feet in length. Here the Jews gather to grieve over the loss of their temple. This wall was the goal of the Israeli soldiers who conquered the Old City during the Six-Day War of 1967.

The Pool of Bethesda—On the grounds of the Church of St. Anne just inside St. Stephen's Gate to the right (as one enters) the Pool of Bethesda can be seen. It is very much below the surface of the present city streets, as are all places from the time of Christ, due to the many times the city has been destroyed and rebuilt on top of the rubble. It was here Jesus healed the man who had lain so long on one of the five porches waiting for the angel to trouble the water (John 5:2–15).

The Church of St. Anne was built by the Crusaders on what was believed to have been the site of the home of

St. Stephen's Gate in old wall of Jerusalem. Here Stephen was martyred while Saul of Tarsus stood by.

Dome of the Rock on Mount Moriah, the ancient Temple area.

Anne and Joachim, parents of the virgin Mary, and the place where she was born.

Solomon's Quarries—Just north of Herod's Gate, between that and the Damascus Gate, is a seven-foot fissure in the natural rock on which the wall of the city of Jerusalem is built. This opening was discovered almost one hundred years ago and found to lead into a vast underground cavern—the famous quarries from which the stone was cut for the building of Solomon's Temple. Thus we read in First Kings 6:7, "And the house, when it was in building, was built of stone made ready before it was brought thither: so that there was neither hammer nor axe nor any tool of iron heard in the house, while it was in building." Being deep underground all sound was cut off during the cutting.

In 1948 the Jordanians closed the quarries because they feared its passages might lead to the Israeli side of Jerusalem. Since the uniting of the city this is no longer a concern and visitors are permitted to view them. This will be of special interest to the Masonic Lodge. Masons regard the first thirty-six hundred overseers, who put the people to work on the stones for the temple, as the first Freemasons. Blocks hewn from the virgin rock have been shipped to many countries for use as foundation stones in Masonic Lodges.

Solomon's Stables—When Herod the Great was rebuilding and enlarging the temple in Jerusalem, he desired to expand the temple area. In order to do this he built up the hill to the southeast of the temple by a series of arches which today are popularly called "Solomon's Stables," although they had nothing to do with the time of Solomon. Thus a huge platform was made to expand the desired area. There are some eighty-eight pillars in these fascinating underground vaults. Holes in the stone pillars indicate that at some time, possibly Herod's or that of the Crusaders, horses were kept here. Because of this huge platform, the southeastern corner of the temple area was lifted 170 feet above the gorge of the Kidron. This corner is called "a pinnacle of the temple" (Matt. 4:5; Luke 4:9).

Jezreel—Near modern Yizre'el in the eastern portion of the **Valley of Jezreel** (see Esdraelon) is the site of the city of Jezreel where Ahab, king of Israel, built one of his palaces (1 Kings 21:1). After the miracle of the fire falling on Mount Carmel and his destruction of the prophets of Baal, Elijah ran before the chariots of Ahab from Carmel to Jezreel—a distance of some 20 miles (1 Kings 18:46).

Next to Ahab's palace was a vineyard owned by Naboth which the king desired in order to make of it a garden of herbs. Naboth did not want to part with the inheritance of his fathers, but the wicked queen Jezebel arranged a plot to accuse Naboth of blaspheming God and the king, and had him stoned to death. Thus Ahab could take the vineyard (1 Kings 21:1–16). However, God sent Elijah the prophet to announce that the dogs would lick the blood of Ahab in the same spot where they had licked Naboth's blood. He also predicted that Jezebel would be eaten by dogs near the wall of Jezreel (1 Kings 21:17–25). The fulfillment of this prophecy concerning Ahab is recorded in 1 Kings 22:38, the one concerning Jezebel in 2 Kings 9:30–37.

The many acts of judgment executed by Jehu, the furious-driving king of Israel, against the house of Ahab took place in and about the city of Jezreel (2 Kings 9:14–37; 10:6–11, etc.).

Joppa—Known today as **Jaffa,** Joppa (its Greek name) was known in Joshua's time as Japho (Josh. 19:46) and was part of the inheritance of the tribe of Dan. It is located immediately south of and adjacent to the modern city of Tel Aviv (the two are now one municipality) and has a recorded history of thirty-five hundred years.

During the time of Solomon's reign Joppa became the chief seaport of Jerusalem. The famous cedars of Lebanon

House of Simon the Tanner at Joppa where Peter prayed on the housetop.

were floated down to Joppa for overland transportation to Jerusalem for the building of the temple. Later, during the time of Ezra, additional cedars were brought here for the rebuilding of the temple by Zerubbabel (Ezra 3:7). Joppa was also the port from which Jonah sailed in a vain endeavor to go to Tarshish rather than obey the call of God to go warn the wicked city of Nineveh (Jonah 1:3).

Joppa was the home of Dorcas, who seems to have become the mother of the women's missionary movements throughout the Christian church. When she died the disciples sent to Lydda, about 11 miles to the southwest, for Peter. Upon arriving, Peter prayed and said, "Tabitha, arise," and the woman arose immediately, and many believed on the Lord (Acts 9:36–42). Peter remained in Joppa at the house of Simon, the tanner, which was by the sea (Acts

9:43). While praying on the housetop at noon he saw the vision of a great sheet let down from heaven containing all manner of animals (Acts 10:9–16). This led to Peter's ministry to the Gentiles of the house of Cornelius at Caesarea (Acts 10:17–48).

The first Zionist pioneers of the nineteenth century entered the Promised Land through Jaffa harbor. Jews from Jaffa moved a few miles north and founded the city of Tel Aviv in 1909. It is now Israel's second largest city (population 350,000).

Jordan River—The Jordan is the only river in the world which flows for most of its course below sea level. It has its source in a grove on the side of Mount Hermon, about 1,700 feet above sea level. In a distance of about 12 miles it drops nearly to sea level at Lake Hulah, or "The Waters of Merom." This area, which was very marshy, has now been drained except for a small wild fowl sanctuary. Much valuable agricultural land has been reclaimed and millions of gallons of water, which previously seeped into the ground, have been saved.

This descent continues another 6 miles until it enters the Sea of Galilee, which lies 682 feet below sea level. From the lower end of Galilee, 13 miles farther south, it begins its winding course down to the Dead Sea, almost 1,300 feet below sea level. Though the distance from Galilee to the Dead Sea is only 65 air miles, the river twists and turns so that it is about 200 miles in length. The river is but 100 to 200 feet wide except at flood time when it overflows its banks.

The River Jordan has witnessed many miracles of God's power. Three times in history its waters have been miraculously stopped. The first was to enable Joshua and the Children of Israel to pass over into Canaan (Josh. 3:13–17). This was when the river was at flood tide (Josh. 3:15; 4:18). Twelve stones were set up in the bed of the river and twelve were taken from the bottom of the stream and set up at

Gilgal as a memorial of what God had so marvelously done for his people (Josh. 4:1–9, 20–24). The second occasion was when Elijah smote the waters so that he and Elisha might pass over (2 Kings 2:6–8). The third was when Elisha wished to return after the translation of Elijah (2 Kings 2:12–15). This became a sign to those who viewed it that the spirit of Elijah rested upon Elisha. It was also in the River Jordan that Naaman dipped seven times and was healed of his leprosy (2 Kings 5:10–14). In these same waters Elisha caused the axe head to "swim" (2 Kings 6:4–7).

John the Baptist ministered at the River Jordan to the multitudes that came from Jerusalem and Judea. Because Gabriel foretold that John the Baptist would go before the Messiah "in the spirit and power of Elias" (Luke 1:17), it is believed the place John chose to baptize was the same as that where Elijah and Elisha miraculously crossed the river on dry ground. Indeed the traditional place from which Elijah was translated is about one mile east of the baptismal spot where our Lord came to be baptized. Here, near Bethabara, John baptized those who repented of their sins and here he prophesied of the coming of one who "shall baptize you with the Holy Ghost" (Matt. 3:11). John baptized Jesus at his request and insistence. Seeing the Spirit of God descending upon him as a dove, John presented Jesus to the multitude with the unique introduction, "Behold the Lamb of God!" (John 1:29–36).

Kidron, Valley of, Brook—The Valley of Kidron is about 2¾ miles long and is located immediately east of the wall of Jerusalem between the city and the Mount of Olives. It seems to have been a favorite burying place and one in which undesirable things were disposed. During the reforms and revivals under some of Israel's godly kings, idols and other materials used in pagan worship were disposed of in the Brook Kidron. Note the following: Asa burnt his mother's idol here (1 Kings 15:13; 2 Chron. 15:16); Josiah destroyed the vessels made for Baal and the grove which had been erected in the house of the Lord, also the heathen altars made by Ahaz and Manasseh in the temple court (II Kings 23:4, 6, 12); Hezekiah ordered the priests to carry all the "uncleanness that they found in the temple of the Lord" to the Brook Kidron (2 Chron. 29:16), also the heathen altars that were in Jerusalem (2 Chron. 30:14).

When Absalom led the rebellion against his father David, the people who were loyal to the king wept as he passed over the Brook Kidron, thus abandoning the city of Jerusalem to his rebellious son (2 Sam. 15:23). How different as we read of our Lord crossing this brook on his way to Gethsemane! (John 18:1) The Valley of Kidron is sometimes called the **Valley of Jehoshaphat** and is associated with the great day of the judgment of the nations (Joel 3:2, 12).

Kirjath-Jearim—A flourishing Arab village about 9 miles west of Jerusalem, Kirjath-Jearim was one of the four cities of the Gibeonites which was spared because of the league made with Joshua (Josh. 9:17).

Here on the top of a hill is the site of the house of Abinadab who kept the Ark of the Covenant for twenty years after the Philistines sent it back from their territory, and before David carried it up to Jerusalem (1 Sam. 7:1–2; 2 Sam. 6; 1 Chron. 15:25–29). The place today is called **Abu Ghosh** and the site of the house of Abinadab is marked by a huge statue of Mary carrying the baby Jesus in her arms. A French monastery was built there in 1924 called "Notre Dame de L'arche d'Alliance" ("Our Lady of the Ark of the Covenant").

Pious Jewish pilgrims used to rend their garments at this spot in mourning over the destruction of the temple. It was believed by the Crusaders to be the site of the village of Emmaus (Luke 24:13).

Kishon, River—Having its rise on Mount Gilboa, the River Kishon flows west through the Plain of Esdraelon. At the base of Mount Tabor the chariots of Sisera were mired in the mud, contributing to their defeat by the forces of Israel

Absalom's Pillar in the Kidron Valley.

under Deborah and Barak (Judg. 4:7, 13; 5:21). Next to this river, as it flowed by the foot of Mount Carmel, Elijah killed the 450 prophets of Baal after the Lord had answered by fire (1 Kings 18:40).

Lachish—Twenty miles inland from Ashkelon is the site of the biblical city of Lachish. This city was important because it guarded the approaches to the Judean hills and Jerusalem to the north and Egypt to the south. Joshua completely destroyed the inhabitants of Lachish in his campaign through the southern part of Canaan (Josh. 10:31–33). Archaeologists have found the ruins of this city.

David made Lachish a provincial administrative center; his grandson Rehoboam strengthened its defenses about 920 B.C. (2 Chron. 11:5–12) and in 701 B.C. it was destroyed by Sennacherib as he found his way to Egypt blocked. One hundred years later the reconstructed city was destroyed by

Nebuchadnezzar (587 B.C.) and was resettled by some of the Jews on their return from the Babylonish captivity (Neh. 11:30). After the fourth century B.C. Lachish declined when the administrative center was moved to nearby Mareshah. It is merely a Tell today, as is Mareshah (2 Chron 11:8), some 3 miles to the northeast.

Lubban—About 17 miles north of Jerusalem in an imposing valley is the village of Lubban. It marks the traditional frontier between Judea and Samaria and has been identified with Lebonah (Judg. 21:19).

Lydda—The modern city of **Lod** is located about 11 miles southeast of Jaffa, or Joppa, and is known in the New Testament as Lydda. It was here Peter healed Aeneas, who had been bedridden with palsy for eight years (Acts 9:32–35). The city was known as Lod in Old Testament times (1 Chron. 8:12; Ezra 2:33; Neh. 7:37; 11:35).

Tradition says that Saint George, the patron saint of England, was born at Lod and that in 303 A.D. he was martyred here for tearing down the anti-Christian edicts of the Roman emperor. The Church of St. George commemorates his exploits.

Magdala—Magdala was situated 3 miles north of Tiberias on the western shore of the Sea of Galilee (Matt. 15:39). It was the home of Mary Magdalene, out of whom Jesus cast seven devils (Luke 8:2; Mark 16:9). Magdala is mentioned prominently in the writings of Josephus; he uses the city's Greek name, Taricheae. It would appear to have been a town of considerable size in the first century A.D. and fortified when he was Governor of Galilee—before his defection to the Romans.

The city fell to Titus during the struggle between the Jews and the Romans in 66–70 A.D. Six thousand of the strongest Jews were sent to Nero to dig the Corinthian Canal and 30,400 were auctioned off as slaves; 6,700 were killed.

Masada—Masada is an immense brown crag about 2½ miles from the western shore of the Dead Sea in the wilderness of Judah. In Hebrew it means "Fortress." It is half a mile long and 220 yards wide. Some scholars think that Masada is referred to in the story of David's flight from King Saul. In First Samuel 24:22 and First Chronicles 12:8 the word translated "hold" is the Hebrew "Metsada." Herod the Great made a fortification out of this huge plateau, surrounding the top with a high wall interspersed with great defense towers. He also constructed an elaborate palace on the northeastern corner. The top was used for cultivation and great cisterns and cellars were hewn out of the rock for the storage of water and food. It was designed to withstand any seige and was considered impregnable.

When Jerusalem fell to the Romans under Titus in A.D. 70, a band of Jewish patriots under the leadership of Eliezer Ben Yair determined to continue the fight for freedom and made their way to Masada. For three years the Romans sought unsuccessfully to storm the fortress. Eventually they built a huge earth ramp up to its walls and set fire to the inner wall of wood which the defenders had built. As the fire burned through the night the besiegers withdrew. The next morning they launched their attack but were met with complete silence from within. Finally two women emerged from hiding to tell the story. Eliezer had warned the remaining defenders of the torture they and their families would receive if they were captured, challenging them to die by their own hand rather than to surrender. Josephus describes the heroic end of Masada in his "History of the Jewish Wars":

"For at the very moment when with streaming eyes they embraced and caressed their wives, and taking their children in their arms pressed upon them the last, lingering kisses, hands other than their own seemed to assist them and they carried out their purpose, the thought of the agonies they would suffer at the hands of the enemy consoling them for the necessity of killing them. In the end not a man failed to carry out his terrible resolve, but one and all disposed of

Fortress of Masada showing Roman ramp and Herod's three-level palace.

their entire families. Oh! victims of cruel necessity, who with their own hands murdered their wives and children and felt it to be the lightest of evils! Unable to endure any longer the horror of what they had done, and thinking they would be wronging the dead if they outlived them a moment longer, they quickly made a heap of all they possessed and set it on fire; and when ten of them had been chosen by lot to be the executioners of the rest, every man lay down beside his wife and children where they lay, flung his arms round them, and exposed his throat to those who must perform the painful office. These unflinchingly slaughtered them all, then agreed on the same for each other, so that the one who drew the lot should kill the nine and last of all himself: such perfect confidence they all had in each other that neither in doing nor in suffering would one differ from another. So finally the nine presented their throats, and the one man left till last first surveyed the serried ranks of the dead, in case amidst all the slaughter someone was still left in need of his hand; then finding that all had been dispatched, set the palace blazing fiercely, and summoning all his strength drove his sword right through his body and fell down by the side of his family." The tragedy was enacted on the 15th of April, A.D. 73; 960 men, women, and children perished.

From 1963–65, under the leadership of Yigael Yadin, professor of archaeology at the Hebrew University, a great expedition labored at Masada unearthing and restoring much of the massive fortifications, storehouses, palaces, churches, etc. What they found supports Josephus's reports. Uncovered, also, were portions of Scripture from Deuteronomy, Ezekiel, and a part of Psalms 81–85. The remarkable and thrilling thing is that these portions correspond almost word for word with the present Hebrew Masoretic text. Thus another link is provided in the testimony of the unerring character of the Word of God.

Megiddo—The Tell of Megiddo lies on the southern edge of the Plain of Esdraelon, the most famous battlefield in the

One level of Herod's palace at Masada.

world. The mound, which has been extensively excavated, covers some 13 acres and reveals 20 cities built one upon the ruins of another. One of the reasons for its importance as a military stronghold was its water system which dates back 2,800 years. A shaft 120 feet deep connects with the spring outside the city walls by a tunnel 215 feet long.

Megiddo was one of the royal cities of the Canaanites, the king of which was slain by Joshua (Josh. 12:21). Sisera and his army were defeated "by the waters of Megiddo" (Judg. 5:19). During Solomon's reign Megiddo was well fortified as one of the important defense posts of his kingdom (1 Kings 9:15) and was one of his "cities for chariots" (1 Kings 10:26). Excavations have revealed stables capable of taking care of 450 horses and 150 chariots. Here Ahaziah king of Israel was slain (2 Kings 9:27). Josiah unwisely fought with Pharaoh Necoh and the Egyptian army at Megiddo and was slain (2 Chron. 35:20–24). The last great battle of this age will be fought at Armageddon (Har Mageddon, Mount of Megiddo) (Rev. 16:16).

Solomon's Stables at Megiddo, fortress city by the Valley of Esdraelon.

Michmash—Michmash is a town in the inheritance of Benjamin which lies east of Bethel and 7 miles north of Jerusalem. Its modern name is **Mukhmas.** Israel's great victory over the Philistines in the early days of Saul's reign began here (2 Sam. 14:1–23), sparked by the courage and faith of Jonathan and his armorbearer. These two warriors took advantage of the narrow, precipitous pass which alone offered access to Michmash. The peculiarity of the terrain is taken into account as Isaiah describes the approach to the Assyrian and his army as he makes his way to Jerusalem. When he comes to Michmash the prophet says he must lay up his carriages—store his baggage—because of the narrowness of the passage (Isa. 10:28). Michmash is among the towns which Judah resettled as they returned from their captivity in Babylon (Ezra 2:27; Neh. 7:31).

Mizpah or **Mizpeh**—The Hebrew permits both spellings of the name of this town in the territory of Benjamin (Josh. 18:26). It seems to have been a prominent religious center particularly in the time of Samuel the prophet. Here the men of Israel were gathered together to deal with the tribe of Benjamin after the incident of the Levite and his concubine (Judg. 21:1–8). Samuel called Israel to Mizpeh for prayer and rededication (2 Sam. 7:5–7). While here they were attacked by the Philistines. In Mizpeh Saul, the son of Kish, was proclaimed the first king of Israel (1 Sam. 10:17–24). Other references to this place are 1 Kings 15:22; 2 Chron. 16:6; 2 Kings 25:23; Neh. 3:7, 15, 19; Jer. 40:8; 41:10.

There seems to be disagreement among the scholars regarding the exact location of Mizpeh. Some hold to Tel en-Nasbeh, 7 miles north of Jerusalem. Others believe it to be Nebi Samwil ("the prophet Samuel"), 4½ miles northwest of Jerusalem, which is the traditional home and burying place of Samuel.

Moreh, Hill of—Mentioned in the account of Gideon's battle with the Midianites in the Valley of Jezreel (Judg. 7:1), the Hill of Moreh rises abruptly from the northern edge of the valley. It used to be called "Little Hermon," but is now known as **Giv'at Hamore.**

Nain—At the foot of the Hill of Moreh, to the north, is the village of Nain (Na'im). Here Jesus raised from the dead the widow's only son as he was being taken out of the gate of the city for burial (Luke 7:11–18). A small church has been erected to commemorate this miracle.

Nazareth—The city of Nazareth lies in the hills of southern Galilee about midway between the Sea of Galilee and the Mediterranean. It is first mentioned in the Bible at the time of the Annunciation (Luke 1:26). It was a rather obscure village, off the regular trade routes. Nathanael's words, "Can there any good thing come out of Nazareth?" (John 1:46) indicates its lack of reputation. Joseph the carpenter lived here and from Nazareth he took his wife, Mary, to Bethlehem where Jesus was born (Luke 2:1–7). After their return from the flight into Egypt, to escape the ire of Herod, they took

One of the main streets of Nazareth. The tower of the Church of
Annunciation can be seen on the right.

up residence in Nazareth (Matt. 2:19–23; Luke 2:39–40)
where the years of Christ's boyhood and young manhood
were spent (Luke 2:51–52).

After his baptism and temptation, Jesus came to minister
in Nazareth. Here he preached his first recorded sermon.
However, the opposition to him in the synagogue there was
so violent that he may never have returned (Luke 4:16–30).
The mountain from which the people sought to cast him is
called today "The Mount of Precipitation." Some believe
that Matthew 13:53–58 and Mark 6:1–6 indicate one later
visit. In these passages it is stated that he could do no
mighty works there "because of their unbelief." Visitors today are shown the Grotto of the Annunciation, where it is
believed Gabriel visited Mary (Luke 1:26–38). Here beneath
the Church of the Annunciation are two granite pillars, one
called the "Column of Gabriel" and the other the "Column
of Mary." Underneath the Church of St. Joseph is the cave

Virgin's Fountain in Nazareth.

traditionally considered the location of the home and carpenter shop of Joseph and Mary.

Of particular interest in Nazareth is Mary's Well (sometimes called the Virgin's Fountain). It is fed from the only
spring in the city and most certainly is the same from which
Mary obtained water at the time of our Lord.

Olives, Mount of—Due east of the city of Jerusalem,
across the Kidron Valley, is the Mount of Olives. Its height
reaches 2,641 feet above the Mediterranean Sea, making it
considerably higher than Jerusalem itself. From its summit
one is afforded an inspiring view of the city as well as the
Jordan valley to the east. The northern of the two main
summits, which is 2,723 feet above sea level, is known as Viri
Galilaei. The chief hill of Olivet is just south of that and is
marked by the Tower of the Ascension of the Russian Orthodox Church; it is visible for miles. The next elevation to the
south is called "The Prophets" because of the presence of
ancient tombs, believed by some to be those of Absalom,
James, and Zachariah, the father of John the Baptist. The

southernmost elevation is called the Mount of Offense, being associated with the places of idolatrous worship which Solomon built through the influence of his heathen wives (1 Kings 11:4–8; 2 Kings 23:13).

While the Mount of Olives is associated with some of the most important events in the life of our Lord, it is seldom mentioned in the Old Testament. David, fleeing from the city of Jerusalem at the time of Absalom's rebellion, crossed the Kidron and worshiped atop the Mount of Olives (2 Sam. 15:30–32). Just past the summit of the hill, David was met by Ziba, the servant of Mephibosheth, who presented him with asses to ride on and bread, raisins, fruit, and wine to sustain him on his flight (2 Sam. 16:1–2).

With but few exceptions (John 8:1 and possibly the giving of the Lord's Prayer) all the recorded incidents associating Jesus with this mount belong in the Passion Week. Of course the incidents described in relation to Bethany took place here inasmuch as Bethany is on the eastern slope of the hill.

From Bethphage Jesus began his triumphal entry going down the slopes of Olivet, across the Kidron and through the Golden Gate into Jerusalem (Mark 11:1; Matt. 21:1; Luke 19:29). Somewhere on Olivet, as the city lay spread out before his gaze, Jesus wept over Jerusalem (Luke 19:41–44). A little church named Dominus Flevit has been erected near the Garden of Gethsemane to commemorate this event in the life of Jesus.

During this week he taught in the temple through the day and "at night he went out, and abode in the mount that is called the mount of Olives" (Luke 21:37). The particular part of the mount was Bethany (Matt. 21:17; Mark 11:11). Somewhere between Bethany and Jerusalem he cursed the fig tree on which he found no fruit and the tree subsequently withered away. This he used as a sign to the disciples of the power of faith unmingled with any doubt (Matt. 21:18–22; Mark 11:12–14, 20–24).

As Jesus sat upon the Mount of Olives his disciples asked the three great questions which drew forth from him the

City of Jerusalem as seen from the Mount of Olives.

Olivet Discourse, outlining the destruction of the temple and events leading up to his second coming (Matt. 24 and 25; Mark 13; Luke 21:5–35).

After eating the Passover in the upper room, Jesus and his disciples went out to the Mount of Olives (Matt. 26:30; Mark 14:26; Luke 22:39), where under the old olive trees in the Garden of Gethsemane Jesus agonized in prayer while the others slept (Matt. 26:36–46; Mark 14:32–42; Luke 22:39–46; John 18:1). Here he was betrayed by Judas Iscariot and arrested by the soldiers (Matt. 26:47–56; Mark 14:43–52; Luke 22:47–54; John 18:2–13).

In the vicinity of Bethany, rather than on the traditional spot, Jesus gave the great promise of the Holy Spirit's power, lifted up his hands and blessed his disciples, and was carried up into heaven (Luke 24:50–51). Then appeared the two in white apparel who spoke of the Lord's return in the same manner in which he went away (Acts 1:8–11). Zechariah describes the second coming of Jesus, when "his feet shall stand in that day upon the mount of Olives" at which time the mount will cleave in the middle forming "a very great valley" (Zech. 14:4).

Although the Scripture does not so state, tradition has it that it was on the Mount of Olives Jesus taught his disciples to pray. The Pater Noster Church has been built on this supposed spot; on its walls are tiles inscribed with the Lord's Prayer in forty-four languages.

Petach-Tikva—Founded in 1878, Petach-Tikva (The Door of Hope) is the oldest Jewish agricultural settlement in Israel. It is named from Hosea's prophecy, "I will give her her vineyards from thence, and the valley of Achor for a door of hope" (Hos. 2:15). The valley of Achor, which is in the Jordan plain near Jericho, is the place where Achan was executed as the result of stealing some of the spoils from the conquest of Jericho (Josh. 7). This settlement, 7 miles northeast of Tel Aviv is named from this event.

Philip's Spring—South of Solomon's Pools on the road to Hebron is a spring of water traditionally associated with Philip the Evangelist and his encounter with the Ethiopian eunuch. Philip was led by the Holy Spirit to leave the revival at Samaria and go south from Jerusalem to Gaza where he met the eunuch reading the prophecy of Isaiah and pointed him to Christ. The spring is on one of the old caravan routes that led from the east through Gaza; it is said that this was the place where Philip baptized his new convert (Acts 8:26–40).

Qumran—At the northwest corner of the Dead Sea lies the site of Qumran, made famous by "the greatest archaeological find of the twentieth century"—the Dead Sea Scrolls. One hot day in 1947 a young Bedouin goatherder, Muhammad Adh-Dhib, was amusing himself tossing stones across a wadi (valley) into a cave. He was startled to hear a sound as though pottery was breaking. Investigating, he found a number of pottery jars containing rolled up scrolls of leather. He took them home and kept them for a time, then spoke of them to a merchant in Bethlehem. The merchant in turn brought them to the American School of Oriental Research in Jerusalem. Eventually other caves in the Qumran area were searched and many more scrolls were found. A number of these may be seen at The Shrine of the Book in Jerusalem.

The story of the Dead Sea Scrolls centers around a monastic sect called the Essenes who lived at Qumran. They apparently believed it their responsibility to copy the sacred Scriptures (in addition to their Manual of Discipline and an account of the "War Between the Children of Light and Darkness"). It is believed that the Essenes, hearing of the approach of the Roman legions in 68 A.D., put their precious scrolls—including a complete text of Isaiah, more than one thousand years older than any discovered previously—in pottery jars and hid them in caves in the nearby hills, intending to come back for them. The Essenes were probably killed by the Romans.

Qumran, showing the large community room where the Essenes ate their meals.

The uncovered ruins at Qumran show every evidence of a detailed communal type of living. Outstanding are the cisterns, a store house, community kitchen, dining room, workshops, a pantry in which hundreds of bowls, dishes, and jugs were found stacked in piles against the wall, and the Scriptorium, where the scrolls were copied. Portions of all the Old Testament books, with the exception of Esther, have been found at Qumran. Copied between 170 B.C. and the early part of the first century A.D., these scrolls have done much to offset some of the criticisms of skeptical scholars.

Safad—At 2,660 feet above sea level, Safad offers a superb view of Palestine. The city is located 10 miles northeast of the Sea of Galilee on the ancient highway from Damascus in Syria to Acre on Israel's Mediterranean coast.

Safad is one of the four holy cities of the Jews, the others

Cave Number 4 at Qumran. More scrolls were found here than in any other cave.

being Jerusalem, Hebron, and Tiberius. Its Hebrew name is **Zefat.**

Saint Peter in Gallicantu—South of the Dung Gate and on the eastern slope of the hill overlooking the Valley of Kidron is the site of Saint Peter in Gallicantu, or the Palace of Caiaphas—Caiaphas was high priest at the time of Jesus' arrest and crucifixion. It was to this place the Lord was taken immediately after the soldiers laid hold of him in the Garden of Gethsemane. This too was the scene of his first trial (Matt. 26:57–63; Mark 14:53–65; Luke 22:54, 63–71; John 18:12–14, 19–24) and the place where Peter denied his Lord three times (Matt. 26:34, 69–75; Mark 14:66–72; Luke 22:54–62; John 18:15–18, 25–27).

The Assumptionist Fathers have built a church on this site which they call "St. Peter Gallicantu," meaning "At the crowing of the cock.' Here can be seen the steps which may constitute the oldest street in Jerusalem, up which Jesus was led from Gethsemane. Also visible is the courtyard where Peter warmed himself, the servants' quarters where the maid who questioned Peter must have lived, and the cell in which Jesus was kept that memorable night. There is also another cell which could have been the place where the apostles were imprisoned by the Sanhedrin (Acts 4:3; 5:17–23).

Samaria—Nine miles north of Nablus is the city of Sebaste (modern Sebastiyeh) known in the Bible as Samaria. According to First Kings 16:24, Omri, king of Israel, bought an imposing hill from Shemer for two talents of silver and began to build a beautiful capital city. He lived here only six years when he died and his son Ahab reigned in his place. Here Ahab built his beautiful ivory palace complete with a temple to Baal (1 Kings 16:31–33). His son Jehoram put away the image of Baal (2 Kings 3:2) and Jehu later destroyed all semblance of Baal worship and killed all the priests of Baal (2 Kings 10:17–28). Jehu also destroyed all of the house of Ahab, including his 70 sons who lived at Sa-

Beautiful columned street of Samaria, capital of the Northern Kingdom of Israel. Now called Sebaste.

maria (2 Kings 10:1–11). Samaria was the burial place for the kings of Israel (the Northern Kingdom): Omri (1 Kings 16:28); Ahab (22:37); Jehu (2 Kings 10:35); Jehoahaz (13:9); Joash (13:13); Jehoash (14:16).

It was to Samaria that Naaman came to be healed of his leprosy (2 Kings 5:3–5). Elisha led the blinded Syrian army, which had surrounded him at Dothan, into the city of Samaria, Israel's capital (2 Kings 6:18–23). Following this came the great seige of Samaria, the terrible famine, and the marvelous deliverance of God which was discovered by the four leprous men who found that the Syrian army had fled (2 Kings 6:24–33; 7:1–16).

Samaria continued to be the capital of the Northern Kingdom of Israel until 722 B.C. when the King of Assyria carried the ten tribes of Israel into captivity (2 Kings 17:3–6, 23). Shalmaneser began the seige but died before the city fell. Sargon, one of his generals, actually took the city and carried the inhabitants away captive. Later the territory was occupied by the Babylonians, Persians, Greeks, and Romans. After the Roman conquest the town was rebuilt by Pompey. Later Augustus gave it to Herod the Great who called it "Sebaste" (Greek for "Augustus").

It was at Samaria that Philip the evangelist was used to bring great revival, and here the Holy Spirit was outpoured through the ministry of Peter and John (Acts 8:5–25).

Shechem—Sitting in a pleasant valley between Mount Gerizim and Mount Ebal, Shechem (or Sichem) witnessed many important events in Bible history. It was the site of Abraham's first altar when he came from Haran to the land of Canaan (Gen. 12:6–7). It was under an oak tree near here that Jacob, on his way back to Bethel to worship God, buried the idols that his family had brought with them from Padan Aram (Gen. 35:1–4).

Joseph went to Shechem to seek his brothers who were feeding their flocks (Gen. 37:13–14); they sold him to Ishmaelite traders who took him to Egypt. Subsequently Joseph commanded his brethren not to bury him in Egypt but to carry his bones back to Canaan (Gen. 50:25). The twelve tribes carried his coffin with them through all the forty years of their wilderness wanderings. They buried him at Shechem in a plot of ground which Jacob had purchased many years before from Hamor (Gen. 33:18–19; Josh. 24:32).

Moses had commanded the children of Israel that, when they had entered the Land of Promise, they should gather before Mount Gerizim and Mount Ebal. The blessings of obedience to God were to be read from the former, while the curses would be read from the latter (Deut. 11:26–30; 27:9–26; chapter 28). This Joshua did (Josh 8:30–35).

Here, in the natural amphitheater formed by those two mountains, Joshua, toward the end of his life, assembled the tribes of Israel to commemorate the victories God had given and to enter into a solemn covenant that they would continue to serve the Lord (Josh. 24:1–28).

Shechem was one of the six cities of refuge (Josh. 20:7; 21:21).

Abimelech, the son of Gideon by a concubine, endeavored to establish himself head over all Israel at Shechem. He slew seventy of his brothers, allowing only one to escape. Abimelech reigned three and one-half years in Shechem, but God brought judgment against him and he was slain (Judg. 9).

Rehoboam, one of Solomon's sons, went to Shechem to be crowned king of the twelve tribes (2 Kings 12:1). Jeroboam, son of Nebat and servant of Solomon (1 Kings 11:26) led a successful revolt against Solomon and became king of the northern ten tribes. He made Shechem his capital city (1 Kings 12:25). This was later moved to Tirzah (1 Kings 14:17; 15:21), and then to Samaria (1 Kings 16:24).

The modern Arab name for this community is **Nablus.** The present city, one of the largest in this area, is a little to the northwest of the old site of Shechem. Nablus is of special interest to Bible students because here is located the Samaritan Synagogue. Inside is the ancient Samaritan Pentateuch reputed to be the original copy of the words of

Moses. (Modern scholars, however, date the oldest parts of this document no earlier than the tenth or eleventh centuries A.D.)

The Samaritans were remnants of the northern tribes who were left in their land when the Assyrians carried the majority into captivity in 721 B.C. (2 Kings 17:6, 23). These remnants intermarried with colonists who had been brought into Samaria by the Assyrians (2 Kings 17:24). The Jews, coming back from the Babylonish captivity, believed the blood of those who claimed to be their brethren was tainted and refused to recognize them. Thus a bitter quarrel and hatred began which led to the erection of a rival temple on Mount Gerizim. The Samaritans claimed that this mountain fitted Abraham's description better than Mount Moriah in Jerusalem. When Nehemiah rebuilt the walls of Jerusalem after the captivity in Babylon, the Samaritans, represented by Sanballat, greatly hindered the work (Neh. 2:19–20; 4:1–9; 6:1–14). The Samaritan temple was destroyed by John Hyrcanus about 125 B.C., but the Samaritans still celebrate the Passover feast every year on Mount Gerizim on the evening before the full moon of Nisan (April).

Shiloh—Shiloh may be called the first capital of Israel for here the tabernacle was set up and the ark of the covenant was kept during the long period of the rule of the judges (Josh. 18:1) Shiloh is in a very central location and was the rallying point for the tribes of Israel for almost three and one-half centuries before its fall (Josh. 22:12; Judg. 21:19; 1 Sam 1:3). Here Joshua divided the land of Canaan among the tribes (Josh. 18:2–10; 19:51; 21:1–3).

A yearly sacrifice was made by the people at Shiloh, and Elkannah came with his wife Hannah. She prayed for a son and dedicated him to the Lord before his birth. Later she brought Samuel and it was here he grew up in the service of the Lord under the high priest Eli (1 Samuel 1). The Lord called Samuel in the night and told him of the judgment that was to fall on the house of Eli (1 Samuel 3).

The wife of King Jeroboam disguised herself and came to the blind prophet, Ahijah, at Shiloh to inquire concerning their sick son. She learned of the judgments of God upon the house of Jeroboam (1 Kings 14:1–18).

A yearly feast was held at Shiloh, at which time the young women danced by the vineyards. During the civil war which came about because of the sin of the men of Gibeah, the tribe of Benjamin was virtually exterminated. There were no wives for the men who remained and the other tribes had sworn that they would not give their daughters to the Benjamites. However, the men of Benjamin were encouraged to hide in the vineyards and catch each one a bride from among the young dancers of Shiloh (Judg. 21:16–23).

It appears from history and archaeology that Shiloh was destroyed by the Philistines about 1050 B.C. after they had taken the ark of the covenant (1 Sam. 4). Jeremiah refers to this as a judgment of God because of Israel's sins and uses it as an example of what the Lord would do to Jerusalem and the nation in time, four and one half centuries later (Jer. 7:12–15; 26:6–7).

Shunem—Shunem (Solem, Sulam) lies toward the eastern section of the Valley of Jezreel, south of Mount Tabor. It was the place where the Philistines gathered their forces prior to the battle with Saul and his army who faced them across the valley from the south at Mount Gilboa (2 Sam. 28:4). Here lived the "great woman" who made "a little chamber" for the prophet Elisha to use on his frequent journeys in that area. Even though the son whom Elisha promised would be born to this woman because of her kindness died, he was raised from the dead as Elisha placed himself upon him (2 Kings 4:8–37).

Siloam, Pool of—The Pool of Siloam is located south of the hill Ophel where the Valley of Hinnom runs into the Kidron Valley. It was originally constructed by King Hezekiah as a reservoir at the southern end of his great conduit. Jerusalem's main supply of water was the Gihon Spring which was outside the wall in the Kidron Valley just below the hill of Ophel; such a location exposed it to an attacking enemy. When Sennacherib, king of Assyria, invaded Palestine and besieged Jerusalem in 701 B.C., Hezekiah had the 1,777-foot conduit cut through the solid rock to carry the waters from the Gihon Spring to the Pool of Siloam (2 Kings 20:20; 2 Chron. 32:30). The Gihon Spring was then covered over from the outside. "Why should the kings of Assyria come and find much water?" the people said (2 Chron. 32:2–4). Workmen began at either end of the tunnel with hand picks and accomplished the remarkable engineering feat of creating this 6-foot-high (on the average) tunnel. When the two excavating parties finally met, an inscription was carved in the wall of the tunnel commemorating the event. In 1880 it was accidentally discovered, 19 feet from the Siloam end of the aqueduct, by a boy wading in the pool. It is translated as follows:

> The boring is completed. Now this is the story of the boring through. While the workmen were still lifting pick to pick, each toward his neighbor, and while three cubits remained to be cut through, each heard the voice of the other who called his neighbor, since there was a crevice in the rock on the right side. And on the day of the boring through the stone-cutters struck, each to meet his fellow, pick to pick; and there flowed the waters to the pool for a thousand and two hundred cubits, and a hundred cubits was the height of the rock above the heads of the stone-cutters.

This inscription was later cut out and placed in the Museum of the Ancient Orient at Istanbul. It is one of the very few examples of Hebrew writing that has been preserved from the period prior to 700 B.C.

The blind man was instructed by Jesus to wash in the Pool of Siloam and he "came seeing" (John 9:7–11). It is believed to be the same as "the pool of Siloah by the king's garden" (Neh. 3:15) and "the waters of Shiloah that go softly" (Isa. 8:6).

Sinai, Mount—The Sinai Peninsula is a huge triangle, 260 miles long and 150 miles wide at its northern end situated between the Gulf of Suez and the Gulf of Aqaba. At the southern end of the peninsula is a mass of granite mountains known as Mount Sinai. The chief peak is Jebel Musa, "Mountain of Moses," reaching a height of 7,519 feet. Part way up its slope is the 1,400-year-old Monastery of St. Catherine, named after a fourth century martyr whose bones were said to have been carried here by angels after her death. Legend has it that Catherine was the beautiful daughter of the King of Alexandria who, after renouncing the religion of her father and embracing Christianity, upbraided the Emperor Maximinus for his cruelties and adjured him to give up the worship of false gods. The angry tyrant ordered her scourged and imprisoned. Catherine supposedly performed many miracles, not least of which was her return to life fifteen times when her father's servants repeatedly put her to death. Only when decapitated did she remain dead. Hundreds of years later her body was found on Mount Sinai and brought to the monastery which from then on bore the name of this saint.

It is the oldest monastery of the Greek Orthodox Church. Christian hermits came to Sinai in the third century, seeking escape from Roman persecution as well as looking to live lives of seclusion as did Elijah and John the Baptist. In the sixth century Emperor Justinian ordered this monastery built so these hermits might have a place of shelter from continued attacks of the Bedouin. The monastery holds a great library of two thousand matchless icons and manuscripts. It was here, in 1844, the German scholar Konstantin von Tischendorf found the fourth-century Codex Sinaiticus, one of the oldest Greek manuscripts of the New Testament. It is now in the British Museum.

Mount Sinai is also called **Mount Horeb** in many passages of Scripture, particularly in the Book of Deuteronomy. It is first brought to our attention as the place to which Moses led the flock of his father-in-law Jethro, priest of Midian. Here, on "the mountain of God," the Lord appeared to

Moses in the bush that burned but was not consumed, to commission him to go to Egypt and lead the children of Israel from bondage into the Promised Land (Exod. 3:1; 4:27). It was promised to Moses, as a special token of God's direction, that he would bring the delivered people to this very mountain (Exod. 3:12); this was fulfilled after the Passover night (Exod. 19:1–2).

Sinai is best known by the fact that it was here God gave the children of Israel the Ten Commandments (Exod. 20:1–17; Deut. 5:1–27). Special precautions were ordered so that no one would touch the mountain when God came down (Exod. 19:12–13). For one year the people of Israel camped before the mount. Here those who had been but a disorganized group of slaves were molded into a nation. Laws and ordinances were given to cover every phase of their lives. Here also Moses received directions from God for the building of the tabernacle. From the offerings of the people this highly significant place of sacrifice and worship was erected. Chapters 32–34 of Exodus tell the tragic failure of Israel in their worship of the golden calf as they became impatient with Moses' long stay—40 days—up in the mountain. However, God heard Moses' intercession and, although some three thousand of the people were slain (Exod. 32:28), God spared the remainder. Moses, in his dismay, had broken the two stone tables upon which the Decalogue was written (Exod. 32:19), but God called him back to receive two other tablets (Exod. 34:1–4).

Sinai is also associated with the great prophet Elijah. After his mighty triumph over the prophets of Baal at Mount Carmel (1 Kings 18:17–41), Elijah was frightened by the threats of King Ahab's wife, Jezebel (1 Kings 19:1–2), and fled southward some 100 miles to Beersheba. Near here he rested and was refreshed by an angel and, in the strength of the meal that was given, he journeyed all the way to Mount Sinai—another 250 miles (1 Kings 19:3–8). It was here God sent the wind, the earthquake, and the fire, followed by the still small voice (1 Kings 19:9–18).

In the New Testament Mount Sinai is used by Paul (Gal. 4:21–31) to refer to a life of bondage to the law, typified by Ishmael, Abraham's son by the Egyptian bondwoman Hagar. It is in contrast to one born after the Spirit. Paul is showing the difference between being under law, as a means of salvation, and under grace. Again, in Hebrews 12:18–24, Mount Sinai and Mount Zion are set in contrast to show the difference between the covenant of the law under Moses, and the covenant of grace under Jesus Christ.

Solomon's Pools—Two miles south of Bethlehem on the road to Hebron are three large reservoirs known as Solomon's Pools. Most authorities are agreed that they are misnamed, in that they were built by Pontius Pilate as part of his aqueduct system to supply water for Jerusalem. There is some conjecture, however, that Solomon had beautiful gardens here and that this may be the spot to which he refers in Ecclesiastes 2:4–6. These huge basins gather the water that drains from the hills and springs in this area and are still used as a source of water for Jerusalem.

Sorek, Valley of—Sorek is one of the narrow valleys which cross the Shephelah, a rocky plateau east of the coastal plain, and which runs from the valley of Ajalon southward toward Gaza. The valley of Sorek parallels the valley of Ajalon to the north and the valley of Elah to the south. This is the area where Samson and his parents lived and where he met and succumbed to the enticements of Delilah (Judg. 16:4–21). Eshtaol and Zorah (Judg. 13:25) were on the north side of the valley while Timnath, where Samson sought a wife (Judg. 14:1–2), is located farther southwest, near the mouth of the valley.

Sychar—Though not mentioned in the Old Testament, **Jacob's Well,** located at Sychar, has become famous since New Testament times because of the conversation which took place there between Jesus and the sinful Samaritan woman

(John 4:3–42). The exact location of Sychar is uncertain; some believe that it was at Shechem, others that the ancient site is at **Askar,** a mile or so northeast of the well. Jacob probably dug the well, which is about 75 feet deep, while he and his family were living near Shechem (Gen. 33:18–20).

In her conversation with Jesus at Jacob's well, the Samaritan woman sought to engage him in the age-old argument between the Jews and Samaritans: "Our fathers worshipped in this mountain; and ye say, that in Jerusalem is the place where men ought to worship" (John 4:20). She was referring to the fact that the Samaritans had built a temple on top of Mount Gerizim and annually kept the feasts of the Passover, Pentecost, and Tabernacles there rather than in Jerusalem. Mount Gerizim is one mile southwest of Shechem.

Tabor, Mount—Cone-shaped and symmetrical, Mount Tabor rises on the northeastern area of the Plain of Esdraelon (or Jezreel as it is sometimes called). Rising 1,843 feet above sea level, it stands 5½ miles southeast of Nazareth and 12 miles north of Mount Gilboa. Tabor is mentioned as a boundary between Issachar and Zebulun (Josh 19:22).

It was on the summit and slopes of this mountain that Deborah, Israel's only woman judge, inspired Barak to gather an army from the tribes of Issachar, Zebulun, and Naphtali. From here they swept down the slopes to battle Sisera and the Canaanite hosts in the great valley of Esdraelon. A heavy rainstorm caused the River Kishon to overflow and in the mud Sisera's chariots became useless (Judg. 4:4–16). It was also at Tabor that the brothers of Gideon were slain by Zebah and Zalmunna (Judg. 8:18–21).

Most mountains and high places were the scenes of heathen worship, and Tabor was no exception; it is mentioned as the site of ensnaring rituals (Hos. 5:1). The mountain is also referred to in Psalm 89:12 and Jeremiah 46:18. It has been the ground of many battles as various conquerors have swept over Palestine.

As early as the fourth century A.D., tradition has placed the scenes of the transfiguration of Christ on Mount Tabor. Thus a succession of churches and monasteries have been erected on this mountain. The Roman and Greek Catholic churches have a substantial number of buildings there now. However, inasmuch as there is good reason to believe a town was on top of the mountain in Jesus' time, it seems improbable that he could find a spot secluded enough to fit the description, a "high mountain apart by themselves," at Tabor (Matt. 17:1; Mark 9:2; Luke 9:28). Many believe a better location would be found somewhere on the slopes of Mount Hermon, the highest mountain in the vicinity of northern Palestine.

Tekoa—The old city of Tekoa is identified by the Tell Tequ'a located 6 miles south of Bethlehem. It holds particular interest to Bible students because it was the home of the prophet Amos (Amos 1:1), who was a shepherd and also took care of small fig trees (Amos 7:14). There are none of these trees in this area now. Josephus wrote that the tomb of Amos was located here. Pilgrims used to come to the area to visit it.

Rehoboam fortified many of the cities of Judah when he became king and Tekoa is mentioned as one of these (2 Chron. 11:6). From here came the "wise woman" brought by Joab in his attempt to make a reconciliation between David and Absalom after Absalom had slain his brother Amnon because of his wrong to Tamar their sister (2 Sam. 14:1–24).

The Tell covers an area of 4 or 5 acres. Though not much remains on the surface to suggest the former importance of the city, shepherds still tend their sheep in the area as did Amos of old. Arab Bedouins live here in underground caves.

Tiberias—Tiberias is situated on the west shore of the Sea of Galilee about 10 miles south of Capernaum—the only city of any size on the lake. It was built around 20 A.D. by Herod Antipas as his new capital and named after the then-ruling emperor of Rome. There is no record that Jesus ever visited Tiberias though it is referred to in John 6:23. The area is noted for its therapeutic hot springs, a fact which may account for the large number of sick people coming to Jesus for healing during his Galilean ministry.

After the destruction of Jerusalem by the Romans in 70 A.D., Tiberias became the seat of Jewish learning and the home of the great sages. Here the Palestinian Talmud, popularly called the Jerusalem Talmud, was compiled.

Capernaum, Bethsaida, and Chorazin came under the judgment of Christ, Tiberias did not. They are gone. It remains.

Zion, Mount—Mount Zion is the height which rises close to the southwest corner of the old walled city. At one time, it actually stood within the walls of ancient Jerusalem. It is held to be one of the most sacred places in Israel because here is located the traditional tomb of King David. Above it is an upper room believed to be on the site of that upper room in which Jesus and his disciples ate the last Passover together and where he established the communion service (Mark 14:12–16; Luke 22:7–13). The room is called Coenaculum, which is Latin for "dining hall." This upper room has also been considered to be the place where the 120 disciples were gathered when the Holy Spirit came upon them on the Day of Pentecost (Acts 1:12–15; 2:1–4).

On Mount Zion may also be seen the large buildings of the Dormitian Monastery which marks the spot where it is believed Mary, the mother of Jesus, died. Roman Catholic dogma asserts that from this place, after her death, she was taken into heaven body and soul, an event known as the Assumption.

A heart-touching memorial to the six million Jews slain in Germany during World War II is found in one of the buildings and courtyards on Mount Zion. It has been called the "Chamber of Destruction."

7

Italy

Italy occupies the familiar boot-shaped peninsula extending from the Alps into the Mediterranean Sea. On the north the land frontiers with France, Switzerland, Austria, and Yugoslavia; its peninsular coastline stretches for 2,600 miles. The country is approximately 725 miles long and between 80 and 135 miles wide except at its northern end where it is 375 miles wide. Italy's population is 56,500,000 and its capital is Rome, with about 2,900,000 residents.

Nearly 100 percent of the population are members of the Roman Catholic Church, though freedom of religion is constitutionally guaranteed. The monetary unit is the lira which is divided into 100 centesimi.

From a Bible standpoint Italy is important because of the influence its Roman conquerors had upon Bible lands and Christian believers. It was an edict of Rome which sent Joseph and Mary from Nazareth to Bethlehem so that Jesus might be born where it was prophesied He would be (Micah 5:2, Luke 2:1–7). It was during the comparatively short time that Judea was under the rulership of Rome that Christ came to earth. Thus when he was condemned to death he was crucified as the Scripture had foretold (Isa. 53; Ps. 22). Crucifixion was a Roman form of punishment. The Jewish custom of capital punishment was stoning. This could not be the means of Christ's death for the Scripture said, "A bone of him shall not be broken" (John 19:36; Ps. 34:20).

The closing years of the Apostle Paul's ministry were spent in this land. After suffering shipwreck on the Island of Melita—Malta (Acts 28:1)—he was brought first to Syracuse, on the eastern coast of the island of Sicily, and then to Rhegium (now called Reggio) on the Italian mainland. Then the ship sailed to Puteoli (now known as Pozzuoli) in the Bay of Naples. It was the best harbor nearest to Rome. From here Paul was brought up the Appian Way to the city of Rome (Acts 28:11–16). Although he was kept a prisoner he was allowed to see his friends and minister to them (Acts 28:17–21). It is believed he suffered martyrdom in Rome.

Rome—In Paul's day Rome was the greatest city in the world, with a population of over one million. Today it has nearly three million and is the seat of the government of Italy.

Actually Rome is the seat of two governments, for Vatican City (known as the "state within a city") is the capital of Roman Catholicism. With a population of 1,000, Vatican City is the smallest independent state in the world; it has its own post office and stamps, its own railway station, newspaper, radio station, cemeteries, and small jail. It issues its own passports. It is the largest owner of capital in Italy, with resources in the billions, yet it pays no taxes to the Italian government. Some sixty-five nations maintain embassies or legations to the Holy See distinct from their missions to the government of Italy. It is the site of St. Peter's, the largest church in Christendom. The Vatican Library is a quarter of a mile long. Among its hundreds

Italy

of thousands of volumes is Codex Vaticanus—one of the oldest manuscripts of the Bible. The Sistine Chapel, the Pope's private chapel, is noted for its famous paintings executed on the walls and ceiling by the great Michelangelo. Outstanding is his depiction of the final judgment.

The city of Rome, situated 17 miles from the Mediterranean on the Tiber River, was originally confined to what is known as the Palatine hill. As the settlement grew, six others were added in this order: Capitoline, Quirinal, Caelian, Aventine, Esquiline, and the Viminal. These seven, all on the east side of the Tiber, give to Rome the nickname "city of the seven hills," even though the highest one (the Capitoline) is only 174 feet high.

Visitors to Rome will want to see the sites and remains of the following: The Appian Way, over which Paul walked as he came to Rome; the Mamertine Prison, where it is believed Paul spent some time; the Catacombs, sacred burial grounds of Christians and the place where they took refuge from persecution; St. Paul's Outside-the-Walls, believed to be the place where the apostle was martyred; the Forum, which lies in a valley between the Capitoline and Palatine hills, containing many famous buildings, arches and temples; the Pantheon; the Arch of Constantine; the Scala Santa, the steps where Martin Luther accepted the truth that "the just shall live by faith"; St. Peter-in-Chains, in which is the original of Michelangelo's famous Moses; the Palazzo Venezia, where Mussolini held forth on the balcony; the huge monument to Victor Immanuel II: the Spanish Steps; the Trevi Fountain, made famous by the movie, "Three Coins in a Fountain"; the Colosseum, not built until after Paul's time; and the Circus Maximus, seating 250,000 in Nero's time.

The time of the introduction of Christianity to Rome is entirely uncertain, nor is there any positive evidence as to who was used to do so. It has been suggested that it was brought here by Jews who were in Jerusalem on the day of Pentecost. The list of those present includes "visitors (from)

The Colosseum at Rome.

The Forum at Rome.

Rome" (Acts 2:10NIV). There was a Christian church here when Paul arrived (Acts 28:15). In fact he had addressed his epistle to them a few years earlier (Rom. 1:7). Paul was permitted to preach while he was in custody (Acts 28:17–24, 30–31; Phil. 1:12–13).

At first Christians were not distinguished from Jews by the Roman officials. However, after Nero set fire to the city and accused the Christians of doing so, persecutions began. Sometime after this it became unlawful even to be a Christian. Persecutions of the Christian church were carried on intermittently until Constantine issued the Edict of Milan in 313 establishing toleration and restoring the property of the church.

8

Jordan

The Hashemite Kingdom of Jordan (previously Transjordan) came into being officially in 1947. In 1950 it was enlarged to include the district of Samaria and part of Judea. The country is bounded by Syria on the north, Iraq on the northeast, Saudi Arabia on the east and south, and Israel on the west. The total area was 37,297 square miles, but since the Six-Day War of June 1967 this has been reduced by 2,165 square miles west of the Jordan River (the West Bank). The country extends south to its only seaport at Aqaba on the Gulf of Aqaba.

The population is estimated at 3,475,000. The capital city is Amman, known in the past as Philadelphia; it has a population of over 650,000. The currency is based on the Jordanian dinar. There are 1,000 fils in a dinar.

In biblical times the area consisted of, from south to north, Edom, Moab, Ammon, and Gilead. The children of

Israel traversed this area as they came up the eastern side of the Dead Sea before crossing the Jordan River into Canaan. The Edomites refused to allow them to pass through their land (Num. 20:14–21; 21:4). This is a reflection of the ancient strife between Jacob, father of the Israelites, and Esau his brother, father of the Edomites. Moab was occupied by the Moabites, descendents of Lot's older surviving daughter who bore a son to him (Gen. 19:30–37). The people of Moab also refused to let Israel pass through their borders, forcing them to go around (Deut. 2:9–11; Judg. 11:17–18). Ammon was the son of Lot by the younger of his two surviving daughters (Gen. 19:38). Moab was the country to which Naomi and her husband went during the famine—Ruth was a native of Moab (Ruth 1:1–4). The country of the Ammonites extended from the brook Arnon on the south to the Jabbok on the north. Sihon, king of the Amorites who lived west of the Jordan, had taken much of the territory of the Ammonites including Gilead to the north. Joshua fought against him as well as Og king of Bashan, north of Gilead, conquering both (Num. 21:21–35; Deut. 2:24–3:11; Judg. 11:19–23). Their land was part of the inheritance given to the children of Israel—specifically the tribes of Reuben, Gad, and one-half of Manasseh (Deut. 3:12–20; Josh. 1:12–18; chapter 22).

Amman—Amman is the capital of the Hashemite Kingdom of Jordan. It was once the capital city of the Ammonites (around 1200 B.C.) and it was called Rabbath Ammon. In the Bible it is associated with the dishonorable act of King David in taking Bathsheba while he arranged for the murder of her husband, Uriah the Hittite (2 Sam. 11). David had intended to befriend Hanan the king of the Ammonites, sending ambassadors of good will to comfort him at the death of his father. Their purpose was misunderstood and the Ammonites insulted David's men by cutting off half their beards and one half of their clothes. This led to the war between the Israelites and the Ammonites (2 Sam. 10:1–19).

The huge Roman Theatre, seating six thousand, is one of the best preserved antiquities in all of Jordan. It was built in

Jordan

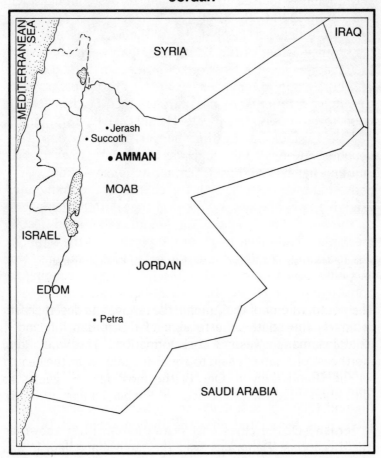

the second or third century A.D. and is still used today. Amman has a population of about 650,000.

Aqaba—Jordan's only seaport and also a resort, Aqaba is located about two miles south of Ezion-Geber at the northeast end of the Gulf of Aqaba, an arm of the Red Sea. It is at

Stage and a few seats of a Roman theater seating over 6,000 at Amman, capital of Jordan.

the southern end of the Arabah, the fascinating desert chasm which is the southern extension of the Jordan Rift and it contains many awesome rock formations. The Wadi Ram, northeast of Aqaba, is said to equal, in many ways, the beauty of the Grand Canyon. One of the most famous guests to disembark here was the Queen of Sheba (1 Kings 10:1–13).

Jerash—Of the cities east of the Jordan River known as the Decapolis, Damascus was the largest and Jerash was second. It is the most complete ruins of a provincial Roman city in the world.

Also known as Gerasa, this city has been called "The Pompeii of the East," and "The City of a Thousand Pillars." Of the more than six hundred stately pillars in the original city, two hundred still stand; seventy-five of them line the city's long main street.

Excavations begun in the 1920s revealed a triple-arched

gate, a huge hippodrome, a theater with a seating capacity of six thousand, the only oval Roman forum surrounded by fifty-six Ionic columns, plus tremendous temples, baths, and public buildings.

The Revised Standard Version connects Mark 5:1 and Luke 8:26 with Gerasa, but it is believed that this is incorrect. Although there is no proof that Jesus ever visited Jerash, he was certainly well known there (Matt. 4:25) and could have visited the city (Mark 7:31).

A few miles south of Jerash one crosses the River Jabbok. It was by this river at Penuel that Jacob wrestled with the heavenly visitor (Gen. 32:22–31).

The River Jabbok was the northern boundary of the kingdom of the Amorites. The River Arnon, which flows into the eastern side of the Dead Sea, marked its southern border. (Num. 21:21–24). To the south was Moab.

Nebo, Mount—East of the Dead Sea in what was the land of Moab is Mount Nebo, from which Moses viewed the Promised Land. It was also here, in a valley, that he died and was buried (Num. 33:47; Deut. 32:49–52; 34:1–8). From Mount Nebo on a clear day the entire land of Canaan can be seen—150 miles from Dan to Beersheba and an average of 40 miles from the Jordan River to the Mediterranean.

Mount Nebo was the summit of Mount Pisgah.

Penuel—Penuel was located somewhere east of the Jordan and north of the River Jabbok. Its exact location has not yet been identified, but it may have been near Succoth. After his remarkable encounter with the heavenly visitor Jacob called the place "Peniel" which means "the face of God" (Gen. 32:21–31). Years later a city with a strong tower stood upon the spot. Because of the churlishness of the inhabitants during Gideon's pursuit of the Midianites, Gideon returned and destroyed the tower and killed the men of the city (Judg. 8:8, 9, 17). After his rebellion and the separation of the northern kingdom, Jeroboam built and fortified Penuel (1 Kings 12:25).

Petra—About 166 miles south of Amman, Jordan, halfway between the southern end of the Dead Sea and the Gulf of Aqaba, is the fabulous rose-red city of Petra. On the way south to this city one passes Ma'an, believed by some to be the scene of the healing of the children of Israel by the miracle of the brazen serpent (Num. 21:4–9; John 3:14). A few miles north of Petra is 'Ain Mussa, accepted by the Moslems as the place where Moses struck the rock and the water came forth (Num. 20:8–13). Today the water still flows generously in an otherwise arid wilderness.

Petra is surrounded by the rugged mountains of Edom. On one of these, Mount Hor, Aaron died and was buried (Num. 20:23–29). Petra was probably the land of the bibical Horites around 2000 B.C. (Gen. 14:6; 36:20–21, 29). Esau, the brother of Jacob, migrated to this area and was the ancestor of the Edomites. They incurred the displeasure of God for refusing passage to the children of Israel through their land (Num. 20:14–21; Obad. 10; Amos 1:11; Ezek. 25:12–14). It could be that the expression, "thou that dwellest in the clefts of the rock," refers to ancient Petra (Jer. 49:16–17; Obad. 3). In Second Kings 14:7 is a reference of the conquest of Edom by King Amaziah of Judah. ("Selah" is Petra.)

About 800 B.C. the Nabateans from North Africa settled in Petra. They plundered the caravans that carried luxuries over the route between Arabia, Syria, and Egypt. The stolen goods were hidden in the caves of Petra. Later they abandoned their plundering but exacted high toll for safe passage of the caravans through the valley. With their wealth they embellished Petra with temples, houses, and tombs.

The Romans conquered Petra in 106 A.D. and added many buildings: temples, baths, shops, market places, and a huge amphitheatre seating three to five thousand people. The huge temples and altars here are an amazing exhibition of artistic and engineering skill.

The valley is entered by the Siq—a narrow defile in the red sandstone cliffs which rise 200 to 300 feet. At some

Entrance to the Siq, narrow defile leading into the rose-red city of Petra, Jordan.

places this narrow entrance is only 8 feet wide. It is less than 2 miles long.

Succoth—Succoth is believed to have been at the location known today as Tell Deir 'Alla. It is on a highland more than a mile north of the Brook Jabbok and 4 miles east of the Jordan River in the territory allotted to Gad. Upon his return from Padan Aram, and after being reconciled with his brother Esau, Jacob journeyed to Succoth and here built a house for his family and booths for his cattle (Gen. 33:17; Josh. 13:27). The place took its name from these booths. Succoth means "booths."

After his great victory over the Midianites, Gideon and his three hundred men sought bread from the men of Succoth as they were faint from pursuing the two kings of Midian, Zebah and Zalmunna. They were refused, but after capturing the kings Gideon and his army returned to punish the people of Succoth (Judg. 8:5–7, 15–16).

On the plain of Jordan were rich deposits of clay especially suitable for making molds in which to cast bronze. It was here that Solomon cast an abundance of vessels to be used in the worship at the temple in Jersualem (1 Kings 7:46; 2 Chron. 4:17).

Succoth is referred to in Psalm 60:6 and 108:7. It is not to be confused with the first stopping place of the children of Israel on the night of the Exodus (Exod. 12:37; 13:20; Num. 33:5).

9

Lebanon

The modern State of Lebanon was created after 1918, first under French mandate, and then as an independent territory in 1941. It occupies a strip of land, 4,015 square miles in area, at the east end of the Mediterranean Sea. Syria borders Lebanon on the north and east; Israel borders the country on the south. Lebanon is dominated by the Lebanon Mountains to the west and the Ante Lebanons to the east. Between these two ranges is the beautiful Bekaa Valley, 10 miles wide and 70 to 80 miles long, a most fertile plain, once called the "bread basket of Rome."

Lebanon has a population of 1,598,000, half of whom live in the capital city of Beirut. Religiously, half the population is Christian and the rest are Muslims and Druses. The country has the highest level of education of all countries of the Middle East.

Lebanon is first mentioned in Scripture in Deuteronomy

(1:7; 11:24) where it is spoken of as one of the borders of the land God promised to Israel. Lebanon is noted for its beautiful scenery and Bible writers often used its beauty and fruitfulness to suggest blessings, both natural and spiritual (Ps. 72:16; 104:16–18; Song of Sol. 4:15; Isa. 2:13; 35:2; 60:13; Hos. 14:5). It was noted for its cedars which were used in the construction of Solomon's beautiful temple at Jerusalem. These famous trees may still be seen on the upper slopes of the Lebanon range, though only a few hundred still exist today (1 Kings 5:8–11).

In New Testament times what is now Lebanon was called Phoenicia (Acts 11:19; 15:3; 21:2).

The Lebanese unit of currency is the pound. These are 100 piasters in the pound.

Baalbek—Running north and south through the center of the country of Lebanon, with the Lebanon range to the west and the Ante Lebanons to the east, is the great fertile valley of Bekaa, once "the bread basket of Rome." Toward the northern end of the valley, and at its narrowest point, stand the ruins of the famous temples of Baalbek. The three temples to Jupiter, Bacchus, and Venus are a reminder that Baal and Jupiter Heliopolitanus were worshiped as triadic deities.

These temples were planned and built by the Romans to outshine all other existing temples of the empire. They are thought by many to be Rome's great attempt to impress the kingdoms of the east and to stabilize their empire against the advances of Christianity. Certainly here was the greatest concentration of pagan worship anywhere in the world. They contain the tallest columns ever built, the largest stone blocks ever used by man, and have been said to be the boldest architectural engineering feat ever carried out by man. The temples were begun under Emperor Augustus and construction was carried on for 250 years.

The temple was entered by a great central stairway, 150 feet wide and containing 51 steps. The first court was built

Pillars of the Temple of Jupiter at Baalbek, Lebanon.

in the form of a hexagon 212 feet in diameter and was fronted by 30 red granite columns. Granite for these and hundreds of others was brought from Aswan, Egypt, some 1,200 miles away. Beyond the hexagonal court was the Great Court, 400 feet long and 385 feet wide. A double row of red granite columns 25 feet high, 128 in all, surrounded the inside of the court. The Great Altar towered 57 feet high.

Above and beyond the Great Court were the 54 massive columns of the Temple of Jupiter; only 6 of these remain. They are 65 feet high and are composed of three drums of granite from 12 to 25 feet high each, held together with bronze and iron dowels packed with lead. The base of the temple of Jupiter contains the three largest stones ever handled by man, called the Trilithon. They are 14 feet six inches high, 12 feet thick and average 64 feet in length; they weigh approximately 800 tons each.

To the west of the Temple of Jupiter is the smaller but more ornate Temple of Bacchus. It is one of the most beautiful and best preserved Corinthian temples in antiquity. Twenty-four of the original 46 beautifully fluted Corinthian columns (each 57 feet high) still stand today. This room is the most pretentious scheme of interior decoration ever produced in limestone. The carvings in the limestone of the entire temple are beyond comparison. The still smaller temple of Venus is mostly in ruins.

In 306 A.D. Constantine recognized Christianity and later embraced it, making it the state religion. The rapid spread of Christianity resulted in the closing of the temples at Baalbek and the outlawing of the cult of Jupiter and Venus. The heathen statues were destroyed and the temples of Baalbek were converted into Christian churches. Later Baalbek became an Arab fortress. It was disastrously shaken by a series of earthquakes in 1158 and almost destroyed. The temples have been strengthened and partially rebuilt in recent years.

Byblos—The city of Byblos in Lebanon is located on the Mediterranean coast 25 miles north of Beirut. In Bible times

Lebanon

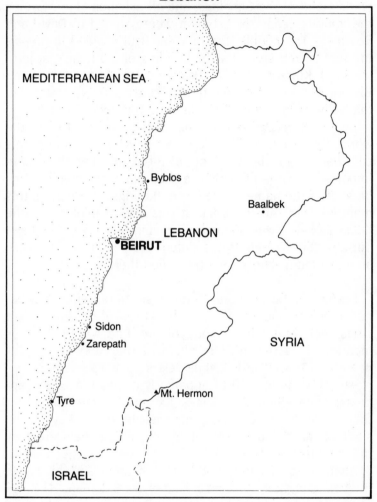

MEDITERRANEAN SEA

• Byblos

Baalbek
•

LEBANON

• BEIRUT

• Sidon
• Zarepath

SYRIA

• Tyre

▲ Mt. Hermon

ISRAEL

it was known as **Gebal.** The Revised Version of Joshua 13:5 reads, "land of the Gebalites, and all Lebanon." From Byblos the famous cedars of Lebanon were shipped to David and Solomon. The people from ancient Byblos aided in preparing timber and stone for the building of the temple at Jerusalem (1 Kings 5:18, NIV). Psalm 83:7 mentions Gebal and Ezekiel 27:9 indicates that the workmen of Gebal assisted in the building of ships for the famous voyagers of Tyre.

Byblos is recognized as one of the oldest cities in the world; its ancient walls date back to 2900 B.C. It is from this city that we get the name of our Bible, for when the Greeks imported papyrus from Byblos they called the material "byblos" after the name of the city of its origin. Writings on this material were called "biblia." It was also at Byblos that the linear alphabet was originated, making this city the home of our alphabet as well. It was called "the book town," because so many manuscripts were published there.

Sidon—Sidon is about 30 miles south of Beirut in Lebanon (ancient Phoenicia). It is the oldest of the Phoenician cities, rich and famous long before Tyre was built. It is mentioned as the most northern of the cities of the Canaanites (Gen. 10:19). Joshua refers to it as "great Zidon" (Josh. 11:8). Judges 10:12 apparently claims that Sidon oppressed the children of Israel. Its sailors were famous for their maritime endeavors, being the first to sail beyond the sight of land, and to sail at night guiding themselves by the stars (Isa. 23:4).

Ahab, king of Israel, added to his other sins by taking Jezebel, "daughter of Ethba'al king of the Sidonians" (1 Kings 16:31, RSV), as his wife. Thus the curse of Baal worship was introduced into Israel. Jesus made dramatic reference to the sinfulness of Sidon and also Tyre (Matt. 11:21–24; Luke 10:13–14).

Through the prophet Ezekiel, God uttered grave prophecies against the wicked city of Sidon (Ezek. 28:21–24). Sidon, though not destroyed as was Tyre, has seen much

Crusader castle by the sea at Sidon on the Mediterranean coast of Lebanon.

bloodshed in her streets. In 351 B.C. the Persians attacked the city and, rather than surrender, the inhabitants set fire to it and 40,000 are said to have perished.

On one occasion Jesus visited as far north as "the coasts of Tyre and Sidon" (Matt. 15:21; Mark 7:24), and here healed the daughter of the Syrophenician woman. Herod received a delegation from Tyre and Sidon at Caesarea (Acts 12:20). Paul, as a prisoner of Rome, was permitted to visit his friends in Sidon (Acts 27:3).

Tyre—Tyre is situated on the coast of the Mediterranean, 30 miles south of Sidon, Lebanon. It was once the most splendid city of the world; it was built partly on the mainland and partly on an island about ¾ mile out in the sea. Joshua 19:29 refers to "the strong city" of Tyre. It was attacked many times through its history but was always able to resist because its ships controlled the sea. Nebuchadnezzar from Babylon once laid seige to Tyre for 13 years; he destroyed the mainland city but was not able to take the island.

A remarkable series of prophecies against Tyre are found in Ezekiel 25:1–28:19. Here Ezekiel describes the famous Phoenician merchant fleet sailing the seas of the world, her pride in her island fortress, and the invasion of Nebuchadnezzar (see also Isaiah 23). Ezekiel 28:12–19 is taken by many to refer to Satan—"the anointed cherub that covereth"—before his fall. The amazing prediction, "I will also scrape her dust from her, and make her the top of a rock" (Ezek. 26:4), was fulfilled when Alexander the Great scraped the debris of the destroyed city on the mainland into the sea to form a causeway out to the island city. He was then able to capture and destroy that part of Tyre, killing 10,000 and taking 30,000 men, women, and children captive and selling them as slaves.

Ezekiel 26:14 states plainly that this city is to "be built no more." Visitors to present day Tyre may wonder about the fulfillment of that prohpecy. If one looks at an aerial view of Tyre he will find that, by the action of the sea, the causeway built by Alexander the Great has become a wide peninsula between the mainland and the former island. This island and peninsula area have been rebuilt many times and there is a thriving city of 60,000 on it now. However, the prophecy of Ezekiel was spoken concerning the mainland city, which has never been rebuilt.

Hiram, king of Tyre, provided cedars of Lebanon for Solomon to use in the construction of the temple at Jerusalem (1 Kings 5:1–12). Solomon also engaged a skilled worker in brass from Tyre (1 Kings 7:13–14).

Jesus visited the area of Tyre (Matt. 15:21; Mark 7:24) where he healed the Syrophenician woman's daughter. The people from this area came to hear him and to be healed (Mark 3:8; Luke 6:17). The sins of Tyre and its sister city Sidon were well known—akin to that of Sodom (Matt. 11:21–24; Luke 10:13–14). Acts 12:20 mentions Herod's displeasure with the people of Tyre and it was at Tyre that Paul stopped and stayed seven days on his last journey to Jerusalem. The disciples here warned him not to go on that journey. Before his departure they all gathered for prayer on the seashore (Acts 21:2–6).

Zarephath—Zarephath lies on the Mediterranean coast about midway between Tyre on the south and Sidon on the north. It is called **Sarafend** today. (*Sarepta* is used in the New Testament; it is the Greek of the Hebrew Zarephath.) This is the place to which Elijah was sent to be sustained by the widow during the latter days of the three-and-one-half year famine. She and her son were also provided for through the miracle of the barrel of meal that did not waste and the cruse of oil which did not fail (1 Kings 17:8–16; Luke 4:25–26). Here also Elijah raised the widow's son to life again (1 Kings 17:17–24). Zarephath is also mentioned in Obadiah 20.

The first Gentile to whom Jesus ministered was a Syrophenician from the region of Tyre and Sidon. He delivered her daughter from a demonic affliction, calling attention to her great faith (Matt. 15:21–28; Mark 7:24–30). It is believed the woman was from Zarephath.

10

Syria

Prior to 1918, the term *Syria* was rather loosely applied to the whole of the territory now forming modern Syria, Lebanon, Israel, and Jordan. In other words, in Bible times it had extended from the Euphrates to the Mediterranean. Today it is much more confined with most of its borders arbitrarily determined. Comprising 71,500 square miles, it has a population of about nine million. Syria borders on Turkey to the north, Iraq on the east and southeast, Jordan to the south, Israel to the southwest, and Lebanon on the west. Its Mediterranean coastline stretches for 200 miles.

The Old Testament records many battles between Israel and the Syrians. There are also times when Syria was an ally of either Israel or Judah. Places of particular biblical interest are Damascus, Antioch, and Seleucia (see related articles).

The Syrian pound is divided into 100 piasters.

Syria

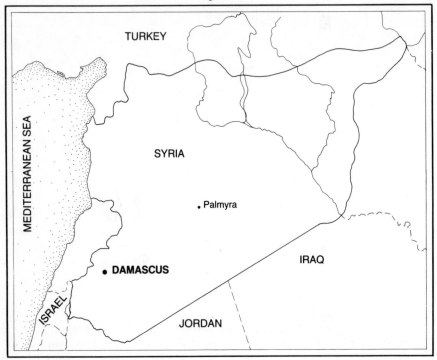

Damascus—Damascus, capital of Syria, is the oldest continuously inhabited city in the world, dating back 6,000
years. It has a population of 1,200,000. In an area dominated
by a desert, Damascus has always been a garden spot for
travelers over the ancient Fertile Crescent. It was a free city
and a member of the Decapolis—that chain of ten autonomous cities which included Beth-shan (Scythopolis) on the
west side of Jordan and Pella, Dion, Kanatha, Raphana, Hypos, Gadara, Philadelphia (Amman), Damascus, and Gerasa
(Jerash) on the east side of the Jordan.

The city is referred to a number of times in the Old Testament. In Genesis 14:15 we read of Abraham pursuing the kings who had captured Lot at Sodom; he recovered his nephew and his goods at Hobah "which is on the left hand (north) of Damascus." In Genesis 15:2 Abraham complains that he has no heir except the steward of his house, "this Eliezer of Damascus." The kings of Damascus were a constant problem to some of the kings of Israel including David (2 Samuel 8:5) and Solomon (1 Kings 11:23–25). Asa, king of Judah, paid Ben-Hadad tribute money to attack Baasha, king of Israel, and thus relieve the pressure on his forces (1 Kings 15:16–20). Ahab, king of Israel, was greatly harassed by Ben-Hadad, king of Syria (1 Kings 20). When King Ahaz of Judah was attacked by the kings of Syria and Israel he sent silver and treasure to Tiglath-pileser, king of Assyria, enlisting his assistance. This led to the overthrow of Damascus by the king of Assyria (2 Kings 16:5–9), a fate which was soon to befall the city of Samaria and the king of Israel.

Damascus is of principal interest to the Christian because of its association with the conversion and the very early ministry of the apostle Paul. It was following the martyrdom of Stephen that Paul (then called Saul), armed with written authority to persecute the Christians, was on his way from Jerusalem to Damascus, a journey of about six days. Nearing the city walls, at the hour of midday, Paul was smitten to the ground by a light from heaven and dramatically converted to Christ (Acts 9:1–19; see also Acts 22:1–16; 26:9–18). Being blinded, he was led into the city where, after three days he was healed, filled with the Spirit, and baptized in water through the ministry of Ananias.

After his conversion Paul spent part of three years in Arabia and then returned to Damascus (Gal. 1:17). In order to avoid arrest, he was let down through a window in the wall so that he might escape (Acts 9:22–25; 2 Cor. 11:32–33).

Places of interest in Damascus for the Christian include: the Street Called Straight, on which was the house of Judas where Paul stayed (Acts 9:11); the house of Ananias, an underground chapel; the window in the city wall where it is

St. Paul's window in the wall of Damascus, Syria.

believed Paul made his escape; the Church of John the Baptist, now the huge Omayad Mosque; the tomb of Saladin, who defeated the Crusaders and conquered Palestine in 1187; the fabulous covered bazaars.

Flowing through the city of Damascus is the River Abana to which Naaman referred when he did not care to follow Elisha's directions to dip seven times in the River Jordan to be cured of his leprosy (2 Kings 5:12). The River Pharpar is a few miles south of the city.

Palmyra—Palmyra is the Latin and Greek for a famous city of the East located about 150 miles northeast of Damascus. Palmyra is called **Tadmor** in the Bible. King Solomon built Tadmor as a commercial outpost (2 Chron. 8:3–4); this gives some idea of the extent of the kingdom of Israel under Solomon.

Tadmor was very prosperous, as indicated by its extensive ruins. It was an oasis in the Syrian desert where the great

Beautiful inner courtyard of a home in Damascus, Syria.

trade routes from the Phoenician ports to the Persian Gulf and those coming up from Petra and South Arabia met. The city collected a duty on all imports and exports. They also enriched themselves by guaranteeing safe passage of caravans through robber-infested areas.

The city was in existence many hundreds of years before Christ, but it was not until the last half of the first century B.C. that it came into real prominence. The imposing central avenue, 1,240 yards long, consisted of no less than 750 columns 55 feet high. The time of the city's greatest splendor was A.D. 130–270. During the Parthian Wars of the third century Palmyra became the mistress of the Roman East. The city actually extended its sway over Syria, Arabia, and Egypt. Because of its revolt against Rome, the populace of Palmyra was killed and the city destroyed in A.D. 272. The city walls and its Temple of the Sun were restored but Palmyra never recovered its greatness.

The Christian Church made considerable progress in Palmyra. The city sent its bishop to the Council of Nicaea in A.D.

325. It was still a wealthy place as late as the fourteenth century, but in the general decline of the East and the change in trade routes it finally sank to be only a poor group of hovels in the courtyard of the Temple of the Sun. The town called Tudmur on the Iraq-Tripoli oil pipelines lies about one-half mile from the ruins of old Palmyra.

11

Turkey

Except for a comparatively small area which lies south of Bulgaria and east of Greece on the European continent, Turkey is in Asia. (Istanbul lies mostly in Europe, but part of the city is across the Bosphorus in Asia.)

Turkey occupies the peninsula of Asia Minor with seas on three sides: the Aegean on the west, the Black Sea to the north, and the Mediterranean on the south. Mountain ranges are on its east, bordering Russia, Iran, Iraq, and Syria. It is 880 miles long and 390 miles wide, comprising 296,000 square miles—a little larger than Texas. Its population is about 47,250,000; about one-tenth of those live in Istanbul (formerly called Constantinople, and before that Byzantium). The capital of Turkey is Ankara, with a population of 2,562,000. Ninety-eight percent of the people in Turkey are Moslems. There are about five hundred mosques, many of them former churches, in Istanbul alone.

The monetary unit is the lira, which contains 100 kurus.

Turkey is very significant to the Christian student of the Bible because of the many places of biblical import which are within its borders: Mount Ararat, where Noah's Ark came to rest (Gen. 8:4); Haran, to which Abraham journeyed with his father when they left Ur of the Chaldees (Gen. 11:31–32); Tarsus, where Paul was born; the cities where Paul preached in Asia, including Antioch and Seleucia (then in Syria), Attalia, Perga, Antioch in Pisidia, Iconium, Lystra, Derbe, Miletus, and Troas; all of the seven churches mentioned in Revelation 2–3 (Ephesus, Smyrna, Pergamos, Thyatira, Sardis, Philadelphia, and Laodicea).

Antioch—Now in Turkey and known as **Antakya,** Antioch in Paul's day was the capital of the province of Syria. It is located on the south bank of the Orontes River about 21 miles from the river's mouth at the Mediterranean; it is 300 miles north of Jerusalem. In Roman times Antioch had a population of 500,000, making it the third largest city in the Roman Empire. It was known as "the Queen of the East." A terrible earthquake shook Antioch in A.D. 526, causing the death of 250,000 people in the province and completely destroying the city.

Syrian Antioch was a very important place in the early history of Christianity. Many believers fleeing persecution in Jerusalem following the stoning of Stephen came to Antioch (Acts 11:19). The gospel was preached here, not only to the Jews but to the Gentiles also. It seems that the church at Antioch pioneered in this departure from tradition. Such was the result that tidings of the revival came to Jersualem and Barnabas was sent there from that home base. He later went to Tarsus and brought Paul to Antioch to assist in the work. It was here the name "Christians" was first applied to the followers of Jesus (Acts 11:20–26). Nicolas, a proselyte of Antioch, was one of the first deacons of the church at Jerusalem (Acts 6:5). Peter was in Antioch for a while (Gal. 2:11–14).

Turkey

BLACK SEA

Mount Ararat

IRAQ

SYRIA

Haran

Antioch (Syrian)

TURKEY

Tarsus

ANKARA

Iconium
Lystra

Derbe

Antioch (Pisidan)

Philadelphia

Laodicea

Perga

Pergamos
Thyatira

Attalia

Sardis

Smyrna

Istanbul

Ephesus

Miletus

Troas

MEDITERRANEAN SEA

The Church at Antioch sent relief to the saints in Judea during the famine in the days of Claudius Caesar (Acts 11:27–30). Antioch became the center of the missionary endeavors of the early church. It was Paul's starting point for his three missionary journeys (Acts 13:1–3; 15:36–41; 18:22–23), and it was here he returned after the first two (Acts 14:26–28; 18:22). The church here instigated the Council at Jerusalem whose decision relieved Gentile Christians of the burden of the Jewish law (Acts 15). It is famous as the birthplace of Chrysostom in 347 B.C. who led the church to its most flourishing period. Archaeologists have uncovered the ruins of more than a score of Christian churches in Antioch.

Antioch in Pisidia—In Paul's day Pisidia was a part of the Roman province of Galatia, district of Phrygia. It was the capital of Southern Galatia. Around 6 B.C. it was made a Roman colony, its citizens thus being awarded Roman citizenship. Ruins of the ancient city are located a mile northeast of the village of Yalvac, 155 miles northeast of Antalya. The University of Michigan has uncovered several buildings of old Antioch.

At the close of their ministry on the island of Cyprus, during the early days of their first missionary journey, Paul and Barnabas sailed from Paphos to Perga in Pamphylia and from there made their way to Antioch in Pisidia (Acts 13:13–14). It must have been a tortuous journey over the rugged mountains which were infested with robbers. Many have thought Paul had this journey in mind when he later referred to having been "in perils of robbers" (2 Cor. 11:26). Here, in the Jewish synagogue, Paul preached the first of the three great sermons recorded in the Book of Acts (Acts 13:14–43). The other two were on Mars Hill at Athens (Acts 17:22–31), and at Miletus to the elders of the church at Ephesus (Acts 20:17–35).

The people of the city were moved by Paul's message, but the envious Jews opposed him (Acts 13:44–45). Paul and Barnabas gave public testimony that they were turning to the Gentiles and many of them believed, "and the word of the Lord was published throughout all the region" (Acts 13:46–49).

Widespread and official persecution was stirred up against the apostles, so they went down to Iconium (Acts 13:50–52; 2 Tim. 3:11). Paul and Barnabas returned to Antioch to strengthen the Christians and to ordain elders in the church before setting sail for Antioch in Syria, thus concluding their first missionary journey (Acts 14:21–26). Paul probably again visited the church in Pisidian Antioch on his second missionary journey (Acts 16:6) and perhaps on his third (Acts 18:23).

Attalia—Attalia (Antalya) was a large port on the south coast of Pamphylia in Asia Minor where Paul and Barnabas landed when they came from Cyprus at the beginning of their first missionary journey. They proceeded from here to preach in Perga, Antioch, Iconium, Lystra, and Derbe. Retracing their steps they sailed from Attalia (Acts 14:25–26) back to Antioch in Syria from whence their journey started (Acts 13:1–3).

Derbe—Derbe was the farthest point reached by Paul and Barnabas on their first missionary journey (Acts 14:20–21). It was the last town in Roman territory on the road running through southern Galatia to the east. There is considerable uncertainty regarding the site of ancient Derbe. It has been presumed to be 16 miles southeast of Lystra in Lycaonia. However, because of the discovery of a column, which is now in Konya, it is thought that the location is about 12 miles north of the village of Karaman which is 66 miles southeast of Konya. The location is called Kerti Huyuk.

Among the many converts at Derbe may have been Gaius (Acts 20:4; Rom. 16:23). Rather than making the comparatively short trip from Derbe, through the Cilician Gates to Tarsus and thence to Antioch in Syria, Paul and Barnabas chose to retrace their steps and again visit Lystra, Iconium, and Pisidian Antioch. This gave them the opportunity to strengthen the churches and appoint qualified leaders over them (Acts 14:21–23). Paul also came through Derbe on his second missionary journey (Acts 16:1).

Ephesus—In Paul's day Ephesus was the capital of proconsular Asia—the Roman province in the western part of Asia Minor. It was one of the three most important cities of the East (along with Alexandria in Egypt and Antioch in Syria) and is midway between Smyrna (Izmir) and Miletus—about 40 miles south of Smyrna. It was built on the Cayster River about 3 miles from the Aegean Sea.

There have actually been five cities of Ephesus; the present town is called **Selcuk.** Ephesus III is the one associated with the apostle Paul's ministry. It was built on the west and south of Mount Pion. At that time it had a beautiful harbor and was the chief commercial city of the east; it was also the wealthiest city in Asia Minor.

Here was located one of the Seven Wonders of the Ancient World—the great temple of the goddess Artemis (Greek) or Diana (Roman). It was said that her image fell down from heaven and the temple was built where she fell. Made of wood, marble, and gold, the temple was 377 feet long by 180 feet wide and stood on an immense raised platform 425 feet by 240 feet. It had over 100 columns 56 feet high and 6 feet in diameter. Little or nothing remains of this great building of Ephesus today; most of what was excavated is in the British Museum. Excavations of the Marble Street, with its many beautiful buildings as well as the great theater (seating some 25,000 people) are most impressive after almost twenty centuries.

Paul came to Ephesus first on his second missionary journey (Acts 18:19–21). He stayed only a short time but returned for a period of two years on his third journey. At this time the Holy Spirit was poured out on believers in a special manner (Acts 19:1–7). Paul preached in the Jewish Synagogue, in the school of Tyrannus, and also in private

Fountain of Memnius of Ephesus in Turkey.

homes, and the Word of God spread throughout all the region (Acts 19:8–10; 20:20). It was in Ephesus that the "special miracles" were wrought by the hands of Paul through "handkerchiefs or aprons" (Acts 19:11–12). God's power was mightily manifest in Ephesus (Acts 19:13–20) so that the worship of the great Diana suffered severely. The uproar instigated by the silversmiths, which overflowed the great theater, testified to the influence of the gospel in that city and area (Acts 19:23–41).

Paul's touching message to the Ephesian elders, who came to Miletus to meet him as he was on his way back to Jerusalem, is one of the apostle's three outstanding sermons recorded in the book of Acts (20:17–38).

The apostle John was one of the early leaders of the church at Ephesus. It is believed he brought Mary, the mother of Jesus, here (John 19:25–27). On Mount Selimisses near Ephesus is a beautiful little chapel built on what some believe was the home where Mary spent her last days. It is called the Panaya Kapulu.

The church at Ephesus was perhaps the most spiritual of the early Christian churches. Certainly Paul's epistle to this church contains some of the most exalted spiritual truths in the New Testament. Our Lord's commendation of this church in the book of Revelation is indeed very gracious (2:1–7).

Haran—In the northwestern part of Mesopotamia (Acts 7:2) is a prairie area called Padan-Aram (Gen. 28:5). Near its center, on the Balikh River (a tributary of the Euphrates) is the city of Haran. In response to God's call, Abraham and his father Terah left Ur to go to Canaan. They tarried at Haran, 600 miles north of Ur, where they stayed until after the death of Terah (Gen. 11:31–32; 12:1–5; Acts 7:2–4). Haran was probably a flourishing city when Abraham was there.

In taking this long circuitous route to go to Canaan, Abraham was following the old caravan roads that led from Mesopotamia to Haran and thence southwest through a great oasis at Palmyra (biblical Tadmor; 2 Chron. 8:4). From there he would continue to Damascas and thence into Canaan where his first stop was Sichem or Shechem (Gen. 12:6). This ancient caravan route, which continues south to Egypt, has been called "The Fertile Crescent." Traders and armies have used it for thousands of years. Canaan thus has been a land bridge between Mesopotamia and Egypt.

Abraham sent his servant back to the area of Haran to find a bride for Isaac (Gen. 24:10). Later Jacob fled here and labored for twenty years (Gen. 28:10; 29:4). Here also he married Leah, Rachel, Zilpah, and Bilhah. All of his twelve sons were born here except Benjamin (Gen. 35:16–19).

Iconium—Eighty miles southeast of Pisidian Antioch, along the military road built by Augustus and called the Royal Road, lies the city of Iconium (now the modern city of **Konya**) in the center of the Antolian plateau—elevation 3,770 feet. The Royal Road extended on to Lystra. In apostolic days Iconium was one of the chief cities in the southern part of the Roman province of Galatia, which at that time included Phrygia.

When Paul and Barnabas were driven out of Pisidian Antioch while on their first missionary journey they made their way to Iconium (Acts 13:51). Here they had great success preaching to both Jew and Gentile. They apparently stayed there for a "long time," but when the multitude of Jews and Gentiles sought to stone them they fled to Lystra, 18 miles south and west of Iconium (Acts 14:1–6; 2 Tim. 3:11). Jews from Iconium, as well as from Antioch, followed Paul and Barnabas and persuaded the people of Lystra to stone Paul (Acts 14:19).

Paul visited Iconium again as he returned to establish the churches and to appoint elders (Acts 14:21–23). He also probably visited the saints at Iconium on his second (Acts 15:36, 41; 16:1–2) and third journeys (Acts 18:22).

Laodicea—Laodicea was the capital of Phrygia. It was located about 100 miles east of Ephesus, just a few miles northeast of the present town of Denizli. It was named in honor of Laodice, the wife of Antiochus II (261–246 B.C.) who rebuilt it on or near the site of a former city. It was destroyed by an earthquake in the first century and was rebuilt by Marcus Aurelius. There was a large colony of Jews there. It was also the seat of a Christian Church (Col. 2:1; 4:13, 15–16). It was one of the seven churches of the Book of Revelation, and its letter is full of awesome warning (Rev. 3:14–22). It is now a heap of ruins called by the Turks Eski Hissar— "Old castle." Remains of the stadium, two theaters, and some of the walls of old Laodicea can be seen.

Lystra—Lystra was a city in the province of Lycaonia (Acts 14:6) 18 miles south and a bit west of Iconium on the Royal Road to Antioch in Pisidia. It was a Roman colony and at that time was part of the province of Galatia. It is on the high tableland north of the Taurus Mountains.

Paul and Barnabas came to Lystra after being threatened with stoning at Iconium. A man who had been a cripple from birth was marvelously healed through Paul's ministry here at Lystra. The people declared that the gods had "come down to us in the likeness of men." They called Barnabas Jupiter— supreme god of the Romans corresponding to the Greek's Zeus—and Paul was called Mercurias, "because he was the chief speaker." Mercury was a Roman god corresponding to Hermes of the Greeks, the son of Zeus; he was regarded as the god of oratory. Paul and Barnabas quickly corrected this attitude. When Jews from Antioch came to Lystra they persuaded the people against the apostles. Thus those who would have worshiped them now stoned Paul (Acts 14:8–19).

Later Paul was to return to this city (Acts 14:21). On his third visit, during his second missionary journey, Timothy joined the evangelistic party (Acts 16:1–4). Paul referred to this young man as "my own son in the faith," and "my dearly beloved son" (1 Tim. 1:2; 2 Tim. 1:2). The two epistles to Timothy form an important part of the New Testament.

Paul may have come through Lystra on his third journey (Acts 18:23).

No archaeological excavations have been made at the site of ancient Lystra; only a few pillars are visible. The site is near the village of Hatunsaray.

Miletus—An ancient and important seaport on the Aegean Sea, Miletus is now some distance from the coast, the harbor having become filled with silt. The village of **Balat** is now on the site of the old city.

On his last journey to Jerusalem Paul stopped at Miletus and sent for the elders of the Ephesian church. When they had arrived he delivered the touching message recorded in Acts 20:17–38. He testified to these church leaders of his ministry among them, warned them of "grievous wolves" who would come among them "not sparing the flock," and told them that they would "see (his) face no more."

This is the third discourse of Paul which is reported by Luke in the Book of Acts. The first was addressed to the Jews in the synagogue at Pisidian Antioch (Acts 13:16–41) and the second was addressed to the Gentiles on Mars Hill in Athens (Acts 17:22–31).

Perga—Perga, modern **Murtana,** was the capital of the province of Pamphylia and a very important city in Roman times. Situated on the Kestros River, it was about 11 miles east of Attalia (Antalya). Its site lies a short distance north of the highway at the village of Aksu, 10 miles east of Antalya. Here may be seen extensive ruins including the theatre, stadium, baths, agora, and basilica. Perga was the first city in Asia Minor to be visited by Paul and Barnabas during their first missionary journey (Acts 13:13). From here John Mark returned to Jerusalem, choosing not to accompany the two apostles any farther (Acts 13:13). After traveling as far east as Derbe, Paul and Barnabas retraced their steps and preached the Word of God in Perga (Acts 14:24–25).

Pergamos (Pergamum)—Now called Bergama, Pergamos is situated 68 miles north of Smyrna (Izmir) and 20 miles inland from the Aegean Sea. Its acropolis rises 1,100 feet. At one time in its history, it was one of the most splendid cities in the Middle East, rivaling even Alexandria and Antioch. Under the Romans, Pergamos was proclaimed capital of the province of Asia.

Revelation 2:12–17 records the letter written to the Christian church at Pergamos. Verse 13 of this passage speaks of "Satan's seat" being here. The great altar of Zeus on the acropolis, discovered by Germans from the Museum of Berlin after many years of extensive excavations, testifies to the city's reputation as a center of idolatry. The altar, 125 feet by 115 feet with 40-foot-high pillars and outstanding bas relief friezes, is in excellent condition and has been transported to Germany.

The excavations on the acropolis have uncovered vast remains of temples, palaces, libraries, and the steepest theater in the ancient world (seating 15,000). The outstanding library contained 200,000 volumes, many of which were written on parchment, a new material invented here and called "pergamena." The library was removed by Mark Anthony and presented to Cleopatra. Nearby is an extensive temple of Aesculapius, the god of medicine. Antipas, called "my faithful martyr" in Revelation 2:13, was murdered in Pergamos. He was the first Christian put to death by the Roman state.

Philadelphia—The New Testament city of Philadelphia (now known as **Alashehir**) is a picturesque town in a narrow valley about 26 miles southeast of Sardis. Built on a terrace some 650 feet above sea level, it was noted for its temples to several of the Roman emperors.

Although its name means "brotherly love," many of Philadelphia's early Christians were martyred. It is said that Christianity was longer taking root there than in some other places.

The letter addressed to Philadelphia in the book of Reve-

A portion of the acropolis of ancient Pergamos (Pergamum), now called Bergama, in Turkey.

lation is the only one containing no condemnation (3:7–13). There is almost no evidence today of the city of John's time. Few excavations have been made.

Sardis—About 58 miles east, and a little north, of Smyrna (Izmir) is the little village of Sart. Nearby are the ruins of ancient Sardis. It is about 36 miles south of Thyatira (Akhisar). Sardis was the capital of Croesus, king of Lydia, who was noted for his fabulous riches. It was he who minted the first coins in history. Christianity was brought to Sardis at an early period as it was one of the seven churches to which letters are addressed in the Book of Revelation (3:1–6). Excavations of the old city have been made by the University of Princeton. Outstanding of these is the temple of Artemis, measuring 300 by 148 feet.

Seleucia—Seleucia Pierria, to distinguish it from other cities named the same, was located about 5 miles from the mouth of the Orontes River. It served as the port of Antioch in Syria—16 miles upriver—and was one of the most important harbors of the Eastern Mediterranean during New Testament times. (Both of these cities are now in Turkey.) Paul and Barnabas passed through Seleucia on their first missionary journey (Acts 13:4; 14:26) and probably returned there on the other journeys. It is now known as **Samandag.**

Smyrna—Now the flourishing city of **Izmir,** Smyrna is located 40 miles north of Ephesus on the Gulf of Izmir. It is the most important port of Asia Minor on the Aegean Sea. The city was recognized as one of the finest cities in Asia and was called "the lovely—the crown of Ionia—the ornament of Asia." Here was located one of the seven churches to which the risen Lord addressed epistles (Rev. 2:8–11). Polycarp, the noted bishop of the church of Smyrna, was martyred here about A.D. 169. The ruins of the Roman agora (market place) take the visitor back to apostolic days. Of interest also is the citadel, known as the Kadifekale, built by

Alexander the Great on Mount Pagos (elevation 525 feet), overlooking the city.

Tarsus—The city of Tarsus was the capital of the province of Cilicia in Southern Asia Minor—now a part of Turkey. It was built on both banks of the Cydnus River about 10 miles from the Mediterranean Sea and 30 miles south of the Taurus Mountains. It was noted in early days for its fine harbor (now closed by silt) which made it an important commercial center. Also, it was on the road connecting the Euphrates Valley to Asia Minor; this road passed through the Taurus Mountains by means of the famous "Cilician Gates"—a narrow pass between walls of rock, and one of the most important mountain passes in the ancient world. Tarsus was also famous for its university, being one of the three principal university cities of its day, along with Athens and Alexandria. It is said to have even surpassed these others in its intellectual eminence. It was at Tarsus that Anthony first met Cleopatra (38 B.C.).

Tarsus is the birthplace of the apostle Paul (Acts 22:3). He speaks of himself as "a citizen of no mean city" (Acts 21:39). After his first visit to Jerusalem, following his conversion to Christ, he returned to Tarsus for several years (Acts 9:30). Barnabas went to get him to help in the rapidly growing church of Antioch in Syria (Acts 11:25). He no doubt visited the city on his second missionary journey (Acts 15:41) and possibly on his third (Acts 18:23).

Thyatira—Thyatira is on the road from Pergamos to Sardis about 44 miles southeast of Pergamos. It was particularly noted for its cloth-dyeing industry. At no place could scarlet cloth be so brilliantly or permanently dyed as here. Paul's first convert in Europe, Lydia, who responded to Paul's message at Philippi, was a seller of purple from Thyatira (Acts 16:14). The Lord addressed one of the letters of Revelation to the church at this place (Rev. 2:18–29). The modern city of **Akisar** now occupies this site.

Troas—Troas is a seaport of Mysia in western Asia Minor. It is located 10 miles south of Homer's Troy, now known as Hissarlik. It was here that Paul, on his second missionary journey, and after being forbidden of the Holy Spirit to preach in Asia and Bithynia, saw the vision of the man of Macedonia inviting him to come and minister there. Sailing from Troas, Paul and his party, including Luke, stopped at the island of Samothrace in the Aegean Sea midway on their journey to Neapolis (modern Kavalla), which was the seaport of Philippi in Macedonia (Acts 16:8–12). This vision, and Paul's response, marked the beginning of his ministry in Europe. Thus the gospel was taken to the West instead of the East. All subsequent history has been affected by this move.

Later, as he returned to Jerusalem on his third journey, Paul visited the church at Troas for one week. While he was preaching, a young man called Eutychus fell out of the window and died. Paul immediately embraced him and the Lord restored him to life (Acts 20:6–12). Note other references to Troas: 2 Cor. 2:12–13; 2 Tim. 4:13.

Bibliography

Harriz, Michel. "A Story in Stone." Beirut: Harb Bijjani Press, 1963.

Keyes, Nelson Beecher. "Story of the Bible World." New York: Hammond, 1959

Kopp, Clemens. "Holy Places of the Gospels." New York: Herder and Herder, 1963

Lapide, Pinchas E. "A Pilgrim's Guide to Israel." London: Harrap, 1966

Morton, V. "In the Steps of the Master." New York: Dodd-Meade, 1934

National Geographic Society. "Everyday Life in Bible Times." Washington, D.C., 1967

Olson, Arnold. "Inside Jerusalem." Glendale, California: Gospel Light Press, 1968

Patterson, Harriet Louise. "Come with Me to the Holy Land." Valley Forge: Judson Press, 1963

Peale, Norman Vincent. "Adventures in the Holy Land." Englewood Cliffs, New Jersey: Prentice-Hall, 1963

Pearlman, M. and Yannai, Y. "Historical Sites in Israel." Tel Aviv: Massadah-P.E.C. Press Ltd., 1965

Pfeiffer, Charles F. "Baker's Bible Atlas." Grand Rapids, Michigan: Baker Book House, 1961

Pfeiffer, Charles F. "Jerusalem Through the Ages." Grand Rapids, Michigan: Baker Book House, 1967

Pfeiffer, Charles and Vos, Howard F. "Wycliffe Historical Geography of Bible Lands." Chicago: Moody Press, 1967

Showker, Kay. "Travel Jordan, The Holy Land." Beirut: Librairie Du Liban

Smith, Wilbur M. "Israeli-Arab Conflict." Glendale, California: Regal Books, 1967

Thomson, W. M. "Land and the Book." London: Nelson, 1888

Unger, Merrill F. "Archaeology of the New Testament." Grand Rapids, Michigan: Zondervan, 1962

Unger, Merrill F. "Archaeology of the Old Testament." Grand Rapids, Michigan: Zondervan, 1954

Unger, Merrill F. "Unger's Bible Dictionary." Chicago: Moody Press, 1957

Unger, Merrill F. "Unger's Bible Handbook." Chicago: Moody Press, 1966

Vilnay, Zev. "Israel Guide." Jerusalem: Sivan Press Ltd., 1967

Vilnay, Zev. "New Israel Atlas." Jerusalem: Israel University Press, 1968

Wolf, Betty Hartman. "Journey Through the Holy Land." Garden City, N. Y.: Doubleday, 1967

Yadin, Yigael. "Masada." London: Weidenfield and Nicolson, 1966

Index